Everything They've Told You About Marketing Is Wrong

71 Things You Need To Know To Navigate The World Of Marketing 2.0

By Ron Shevlin

COVER ART DESIGNED AND PRODUCED BY BRENT DIXON

Cover art by Brent Dixon

Library of Congress Cataloging-in-Publication Data

Shevlin, Ron

  Everything They've Told You About Marketing Is Wrong / Ron Shevlin

    p.cm.

   ISBN-13 978-0-6151-9184-3

Dedicated to Nancy, Lauren, Kristen and Kaitlyn.
The ideas captured in this book
would never have come about without them.

TABLE OF CONTENTS

INTRODUCTION: IT DON'T COME EASY

SECTION 1: STRATEGIC CONSIDERATIONS

SECTION 2: ORGANIZATIONAL DYNAMICS

SECTION 3: ROI MEASUREMENT AND REPORTING

SECTION 4: CUSTOMER EXPERIENCE MANAGEMENT

SECTION 5: CUSTOMER ENGAGEMENT

SECTION 6: CUSTOMER LIFETIME VALUE

SECTION 7: NET PROMOTER SCORE

SECTION 8: CUSTOMER LOYALTY

SECTION 9: WEB 2.0

EPILOG: CLOSING THOUGHTS

NOTES

INTRODUCTION: IT DON'T COME EASY

If you don't know who Ringo Starr is, put this book down, and ask your Mom or Dad to send it back and get a refund. Ringo is important to this book, because he's the guy who sang what could probably be the theme song for this book, "It Don't Come Easy."

You got to pay your dues if you want to sing the blues
Cuz' you know it don't come easy
And this trouble vine keeps growing all the time
Cuz' you know it just ain't easy."

Word. Despite what the gurus -- with their three easy steps, one ultimate question, and cutesy-wutesy titles -- tell you, there's no easy way to succeed in marketing today. There's no silver bullet to attract and retain customers, drive profitability and growth, and help you keep your job for more than the 23 months that today's typical Chief Marketing Officer is in the job for.

The press and blogosphere are all agog with talk of revolution in the world of marketing. It's a complex, fast-changing business world (because, hey, that's what everybody says it is, so it must be true). Web 2.0, social media, social networking, blogging, microblogging, etc. all contributing to what pundits call Marketing 2.0.

There's just one problem -- few firms have yet to figure how to succeed in the world of Marketing 1.0. And if that wasn't bad enough, there's simply a lot of bad advice about Marketing 2.0 out there.

This book won't educate you about the new trends in marketing. It's going to cut through the morass of poorly described, poorly conceived ideas floating around there. Tell it like it is, and tell you what it means.

If 71 steps to success are too many for you, fine -- I'll boil it down to the three things you have to do to keep your job: 1) Cut through the consultant/vendor hype; 2) Figure out what *really* drives growth and profitability in your business; and 3) Focus on *only* those things!

Piece of cake, no? If you'd like to learn about *how* to accomplish those three imperatives, then you'll have to read on.

My goal for this book is that it helps you become a more successful marketer. My hope is that it does that in an entertaining and thought-provoking manner.

The book is organized into nine sections starting off with strategic considerations, addressing organizational issues (including the role of the Chief Marketing Officer), and ROI measurement and reporting. Sections 4 through 9 turn the view outward to cover specific topics like customer experience management, customer engagement, customer lifetime value, net promoter scores, customer loyalty, and Web 2.0.

If focusing on the internal issues and *then* discussing the external forces seems backwards to you, then read the book in any order you choose. As long as you read it all, you won't lose anything in the process.

You'll notice that some chapter titles start with a ☺. These are entries I think of as humor breaks. After all, we're going to need a little levity to get us through this age of mass confusion.

So thanks in advance for reading this book. If there's anything you feel compelled to critique, argue with, or simply respond to, don't hesitate to contact me at ron.shevlin@gmail.com.

And please visit my blog at http://marketingroi.wordpress.com. I'm not figuring on getting rich from this book. So the least I can get out of this is a better Technorati ranking.

SECTION 1: STRATEGIC CONSIDERATIONS

The ~~Four~~ Three P's Of Marketing

Pick up any textbook on marketing and you're sure to read about the four P's of marketing: product, place, price, and promotion. These have been the foundation upon which marketing education has relied for forty or so years.

Most marketing departments, however, only practice three Ps of marketing (and different ones than the textbooks preach, at that): 1) Predicting what customers will buy; 2) Pushing a bunch of marketing messages out to those customers/prospects; and 3) Praying for a better response and conversion rate than the last campaign.

The emergence of new tools and concepts contributing to Marketing 2.0 -- search engine optimization, behavioral targeting, viral marketing, and social networking to name a few -- require marketers to not just understand and utilize these new vehicles, but to develop a whole new competency. I call it a sense-and-respond marketing competency:

"The ability to sense consumer needs and intentions based on their behaviors and actions, and to respond with appropriate advice, guidance, and offers."

When addressing the core competency question, marketing execs must assess how well their marketing department can:

- Sense where a customer is in the buying cycle based on the clues that they provide through in-person, call center, and online interactions;

- Alter the sequence, quantity, and content of messages based on those clues; and

- Respond within an appropriate timeframe (this does not always have to be "real-time") and through the appropriate channels.

The predictive ability that many firms have developed in the past will certainly support them going forward. But what's needed isn't simply the ability to predict *product* need but the ability to predict *message* need (awareness message, advice message, sales message).

Good salespeople have a sense-and-respond capability. They look and listen to their prospect and then respond and guide the prospect through the steps of the buying process.

Marketing has a new imperative in the Marketing 2.0 era: Improve its ability to move customers through the buying cycle with a sense-and-respond capability.

Examples of this new capability include:

- When a customer logs on to check her checking account balance, behind the scenes (all automated, of course) the bank checks the balance, the date, and whether or not the customer has direct deposit. If the customer has direct deposit, the balance is below a certain level, and the date is so many days away from the next deposit, then the site displays a link for a direct deposit advance. The bank claims that this has been the most successful online marketing tactic it has ever deployed. Ever.

- To determine where prospects are in the purchase/decision cycle, a mortgage provider offers a tool on its site that lets prospects compare good faith estimates from other lenders against its own offer -- even though it might not be as good as the other lender's offer. But the market intelligence it gains -- understanding where site visitors are in the purchase cycle, which lenders they're talking to, and what those competitive offers are -- outweighs the potential downside.

- Having relied on demographic data for years to predict need for their home and auto insurance products, one insurer found that type of data insufficient to help it predict the right time to make an offer. Using new mover data, the insurer identified prospects likely to be approaching their renewal date on competitors' policies. Making offers closer to their prospects' renewal dates improved offer response rates significantly.

The challenge for marketers in the world of Marketing 2.0 is systematizing these capabilities -- and not just deploying them as one-off tactics.

Is It In-bound Or In-terruption Marketing?

It would be easy to confuse a sense-and-respond competency with what many call inbound marketing. Fifty-eight percent of the firms Forrester Research surveyed in 2005 said they practice inbound marketing, while another 27% planned to do so by the end of 2006.[1] But what are these firms *really* doing?

One man's inbound marketing message may very well be someone else's interruption -- like when you call your credit card provider to activate your card, but can't complete the call until the rep goes through her cross-sell pitches.

There's no simple answer to this dilemma — many marketers know that their customers are the best candidates to respond to sales pitches. What marketers need to perfect is not inbound marketing, but sense-and-respond marketing.

Building a sense-and-respond marketing competency requires marketers to:

- **Understand context.** Forrester's research discovered that, among consumers who researched credit cards online, more used the Web to confirm the choice of product and provider that had already made, than those who used the Web to find a card from a set of providers they had already selected, or to find a card from a firm they hadn't previously considered. Defining the context for an inbound interaction — e.g., problem resolution, status checking, product exploration, product validation — helps determine what type of message (if any) is the most appropriate.

- **Find demographic predictors.** Demographics can help predict context. For example, when it comes to financial products, women are more likely to go online to validate their choices, while men are more likely to be exploring. Demographic differences apply to call center interactions, as well. Older consumers are willing to spend more time on the phone, and be more tolerant of irrelevant offers. Affluent boomers, on the other hand, don't particularly like to use the phone in the first place, and don't want their time wasted. With their increasing use of the Web to shop, access financial accounts, and self-serve, making cross-sell offers online may be a more effective way to reach these consumers.

- **Mine customer data for trends and insights.** USAA discovered that many customers who cancelled multiple products at one time were doing so not because of any dissatisfaction with the products or the firm, but because they were going through a divorce. This insight led it to change call center reps' scripts from trying to dissuade customers from cancelling insurance policies and credit cards to offering divorce-related services. The result: Customers who remained loyal after their divorce.

The common threads in building a sense-and-respond marketing competency? Understanding the context of the inbound interaction to ensure relevant responses, and the ability to draw upon and analyze customer data to improve the firm's ability sense the context of the interaction.

What it takes to develop a sense-and-respond capability is counter-intuitive. Suppressing a cross-sell offer to complete a call in a more expeditious manner may build goodwill with the customer and *increase* the likelihood that she will do more business in the future. Interrupting the call with an offer may have the opposite effect.

An inbound marketing capability is not what marketers should be striving for -- sense-and-respond is what's needed.

Smart Marketers Focus On Operational Excellence

Not focusing on fixing the problem at hand leads many customers to become suspicious of firms' intention. But the fact that there's a problem in the first place is even more troubling for many consumers.

This is especially true among a segment of consumers I call the Crankys: Relatively well-to-do, highly-educated Boomers (and some Seniors and Gen Xers) who are dissatisfied with many of the firms they interact with. They're not dissatisfied because they get bad service, but because they need service in the first place.

There's a geeky consulting term for this: Operational excellence.

This isn't the same thing as convenience. Convenience is having a branch on every corner, or giving customers the ability to check their account balances online at 11pm while they're wearing their bathrobes.

Operational excellence is something different. This story (from a participant in a market research study) will help describe the difference:

"In addition to the checking account I have with my primary bank, I have a brokerage account with a few stocks (it's not my primary brokerage account). About two months ago, I received a check for $50 from the bank, with no description of why.

When I called the bank to ask why they sent the check, I was told my brokerage account was erroneously charged a $50 custodial fee.

After a brief pause, the rep said that he didn't see the charge on my account. He concluded that the check was erroneously sent. He told me to rip it up and we'd be square. I said fine.

A week later, I got a call from the account manager at my branch (the guy who calls every three months to ask "is everything all right?"). He asked me if I wanted to schedule an appointment with an investment advisor to discuss my portfolio allocation.

I thought "if you guys can't keep $50 straight, how the hell are you going to keep $500,000 straight?" But I said "no, thanks" and hung up. Oh, by the way — I cashed the check anyway."

Is this an example of poor product quality? No. Poor service quality? Not exactly. The Crankys are tired of doing business with firms that make mistakes, don't have their act together, and aren't coordinated across their LOBs — firms that take too much effort on the part of the customer to deal with.

You may be thinking: "OK, but this isn't marketing's problem." It is. The customer experience IS marketing's job. And when back office issues touch the customer, and diminish the customer experience, then smart marketers (who want to stay employed) will get involved.

To the Crankys, a superior customer experience isn't about friendly, helpful people (they didn't want to have to talk to them in the first place), or engaging, interactive ads. It's about fast, seamless, problem-free, defect-free execution.

What it means: Improving profitability requires a renewed focus on process improvement — not only in marketing, but across the firm.

Implications: Marketers should spend less time and money on branding efforts, more on process quality and integration.

Rewards: 1) The Crankys' business and loyalty; 2) Improved brand rankings from customers that experience the operational effectiveness that other firms lack; 3) CEOs who think that marketing is focusing on the right things; and 4) Another year on the job.

Marketing's Civil War

Spending less time and money on media-related branding efforts, and more on process quality and integration challenge to the way traditional marketers think.

One blogger asks if we're in the midst of a culture clash between branding and measurement. The answer is yes — and in financial services, it's more than just a culture clash — it's a civil war within marketing. And there's no question in my mind that branding is winning. How else could you explain the following from Direct magazine:[2]

"Scotiabank figured out how to measure the impact of its brand advertising." Since it already had a handle on direct mail and email, the bank measured the success of TV, print, and outdoor ads in driving consumers to its web site to sign up for a plasma TV giveaway. Since no direct mail or email was sent, site visitors who registered for the contest were credited to the TV spots. Scotiabank has joined the parade of brands that's trying to bring direct marketing's accountability to brand advertising."

No mention of how many sweepstakes entrants became customers, mind you.

At first, I couldn't believe that someone at the bank would say it "had a handle on direct mail and email." But then I realized that if it was a quote, it probably came from a branding warrior being dismissive of the direct channels.

But — as financial firms move from gross to net measurement to gauge the success of their direct marketing efforts — it boggles the mind that Marketing at Scotiabank can get away with this kind of justification on its ad spend, and would even flaunt it as a measure of brand accountability.

Anybody can give away plasma TVs. *N-E-Bah-Dee*.

That branding is winning this war is somewhat of a paradox, when you consider that many execs — especially CFOs — want better quantitative justification for marketing investments. But they don't "get" analytics and database marketing like they "get" advertising. After all, everybody is an advertising expert.

Can the measurement/database marketing army stay in the game and make it a fight? Sure. The "Competing On Analytics" Harvard Business Review article and book by Tom Davenport helps — but only slightly. While a number of analytic-types I know see this as proof (hope?) that analytics can rise to the strategic level, I'm not so optimistic. I think it's more likely that the branding folks will find a way to hijack the term "analytics", throw away the "brand equity" moniker, and start talking about "brand analytics."

What will happen in many firms is what happens in real-life civil wars — one side turns to outside assistance to help fight the war. Where database marketers will turn — or should turn — depends on whether their firm is marketing-, sales-, or finance-driven.

In sales-driven firms, smart database marketers will enlist Sales' help. It won't be easy, of course, if Sales isn't happy with the quantity, quality, and distribution of leads generated today. Improving on these areas can be one way for the database marketers to gain Sales' support to fight the battle with branding. In finance-driven firms, database marketing will align with the CFO organization. Again, the analytic side may have some credibility-building to do.

But enlisting outside help risks exposing the internal battles within Marketing, airing its dirty laundry to the rest of the organization. And credibility-building efforts may take more time than some have the patience for.

In financial firms that are already marketing-driven, I'm not at all optimistic that the analytics side can win the budget and justification battles. In these firms, it will likely take a drop in sales and profitability to force a change in culture and org structure to give analytics a shot at winning. And if that does happen, I'd still bet that the firm either brings in a new CMO from the outside, or promotes someone internally from a completely different function.

On top of all this, remember — this is just one aspect to marketing's civil war. It doesn't even address the warring factions within the branding camp, who fight over the distinctions between "branding" and "the brand."

☺ The Emerging New Consumer Segment: The Crankys

I've been accused of being cranky. I might not be alone. I could be part of a whole segment of cranky consumers. Some evidence:

- **Cranky.com**. Eon's new search engine designed specifically for aging baby boomers. (#1 search term: "sex", #9: "arthritis").

- **MrCranky.com.** Movie reviews with a rating scale that starts with "almost tolerable" and goes down from there to "so godawful that it ruptured the very fabric of space and time with the sheer overpowering force of its mediocrity."

- **The Cranky Product Manager.** A blog from the "the fictional, snarky alter-ego of a mild-mannered software product management professional."

- **Cranky Middle Manager.** An "irreverent but insightful look into the world of middle management."

- **Cranky Literary Journal.** A journal with a "tendency toward quirky writing — work with an unusual or ever-so-slightly skewed perspective. Ironic, but not always, because every so often we have a moment of utterly sincere sentiment."

- **The Cranky Professor** who says he (she?) can be "emailed by carefully retyping without the spaces and with a substituted symbol for the word 'at' and punctuation mark for the word 'dot' at professor at crankyprofessor dot com. If you, too, were a professor you might understand WHY I go into such detail."

And the list goes on. With 78 million baby boomers out there, I guess not all of us can be happy and cheerful (all the time, at least).

SECTION 2: ORGANIZATIONAL DYNAMICS

Delusions Of Marketing Grandeur

Periods of change cause organizational change, and many marketers want to know how to organize to succeed. I've learned a lesson over the past 25 years: Org structure doesn't matter. Any structure will work as long as there's alignment in goals and culture, and internal relationships between executives and departments are established.

It's more important for marketers in this era to understand the leadership requirements they need to succeed, and -- even more importantly -- how to get along with other execs and departments in the firm.

Cuz' guess what? There ain't a lot of firms out there that are marketing-driven. Marketing doesn't have the luxury of being the leading force. Instead, in the sales- and finance-driven firms within which they work, marketers are going to have prove the value of what they do and in what they invest.

An article on MarketingProfs.com stated:[3]

"More and more companies are attempting to become "marketing focused/led" rather than sales or financially driven....A bona fide, world-class marketing-led organization has a clear long-term focus on core items such as retention, customer satisfaction, customer experience management, and lifetime value of a customer. Conversely, a sales- or financially driven organization is primarily focused on acquisition, revenue, market share, and price/costs."

My take: I beg to differ. CMOs that think that they can change the prevailing culture of their organization may be suffering from delusions of marketing grandeur. World-class marketing organizations: 1) maximize their contribution within their firms' culture, and 2) focus on retention, satisfaction, etc. and acquisition, revenue, share, and price/costs.

Where does marketing come off thinking its job is to change the prevailing culture of the firm? CMOs that struggle to demonstrate the ROI of their marketing investments are ill-advised to change the culture of the organization (unless the business is seriously dire straits, but that describes few companies).

Which is not to say that marketing shouldn't advocate for understanding and meeting customer needs, providing excellent customer service, and delivering a great customer experience. But a firm doesn't have to be marketing-driven to deliver on all that.

Marketers gain credibility within their firms when they speak the language that the powers that be speak — and if the prevailing language is acquisition, revenue, share, and profitability, then that's the language marketing should be speaking.

The Future Of The Chief Marketing Officer

What's the biggest problem CMOs have? In my opinion, it's that they're held accountable for too many things for which they have no control, let alone influence, over. The CMO Council might agree. As reported in AdWeek:[4]

"CMOs are failing at a high rate because they lack the skill sets, credibility, and authority to fulfill their often ill-defined jobs."

What does this mean for the future of CMOs?

I believe the evolution of the CMO position will be similar to what has happened with the CIO (chief information officer) position in many firms.

Twenty-five years ago or so, many of the first batch of CIOs were VPs of IT promoted into the senior ranks. Many were great technologists, but few were great strategists or politicians.

So many firms named up-and-coming execs from other functions as CIO. The successful ones raised the technology IQ of the organization, made IT more strategic, and helped to integrate IT with other business functions.

More recently, many newly-appointed CIOs are, again, coming from the ranks of IT. Four factors are contributing to this trend: 1) processes are in place to align business and IT strategies [or at least try to]; 2) senior execs are more comfortable with IT; 3) IT itself is more business savvy; and 4) the technology environment has grown so complex that the CIO position again requires someone with a strong technology background.

The history of the CIO will repeat itself with the CMO.

Dissatisfaction with marketing will lead to the appointment of non-marketing folks into the role. Over time, if successful, they'll help make marketing more strategic and better integrated (not just with other functions, but with itself), paving the way for CMOs tol once again come from the ranks of marketing.

This isn't going to happen overnight, and certainly not in every firm. The success of the non-marketing CMOs will come mostly from their political and managerial abilities, not their marketing acumen. And also from their ability to integrate marketing itself and quell the growing civil war within marketing.

Knuckle-Draggin' CMOs

Forrester Research and Heidrick & Struggles released a report they called The Evolved CMO.[5] I find it odd that they would hold out the model CMO as an "evolved" CMO. That paints a picture of most CMOs as knuckle-draggin' cavemen types from the Stone Age. (Maybe that was intentional). Seems to me that there's a better label to connote the CMO they're trying to describe ("catalytic" comes to mind).

Some of the findings involved CMOs':

1. Top marketing objectives. Number one was acquiring new customers, listed by just over 60% of respondents. But only about one-third listed increasing customer retention. And less than 30% of the senior marketers surveyed said increasing customer lifetime value is a top marketing objective.

My take: This is a worrisome finding. Increasing customer lifetime value should be towards the top of the list. A coherent and effective strategy for increasing CLV will result in the acquisition of profitable new customers, guide customer retention tactics, and help marketing better measure the impact of its efforts and investments.

2. Views on the skills important to their personal success. Vision and strategic thinking was cited by more than three-quarters of marketers as the most important skill/competency. When asked about self-improvement areas, of the 17 attributes listed, the most popular area was "personal knowledge of your customers" and the third most popular was "technology-savviness." But customer knowledge was only mentioned as an important skill by about 10% of respondents, and technology-savviness by less than 20%.

My take: There's a disconnect here. On one hand "strategic thinking" is listed as the most critical skill, but only 16% desire self-improvement in this area. Which implies that they think they've got this nailed down. And the attributes that rose toward the top of the self-improvement list — customer knowledge and technology-savviness — were ranked towards the bottom of the importance list. If they're not very important, then why do so many CMOs want to improve in those areas?

3. Career development resources. From a list of 16 resources to help CMOs build their skills and competencies, marketing publications, conferences, and organizations were ranked at the bottom. Among CMOs, 40% found marketing conferences to be of little to no value — just 10% said they were of great value.

My take: No surprise here. It would be interesting to know, though, why so many (40%) marketers see great value in business publications, but so few (~15%) see great value in marketing publications.

4. Marketing tools and tactics. When asked which tools and tactics are the most important to their marketing organization's future success, the top three are: 1) customer trends and research; 2) marketing measurement; and 3) CRM/customer data analytics. Despite all the hype, social computing/Web 2.0 was second from the bottom, just ahead of user-generated content [note to self: resist urge to call UGC "dumb"].

My take: Many CMOs are missing something here. Social computing and customer community development are techniques to help them better understand customer trends and do customer research.

The next few years will be interesting times for CMOs. I hope I get to work with the ones that walk upright.

The Fourth Skill

Somebody screwed up. I don't know who, and I really don't care, because as a result of this screw-up, I'm sitting in first class on my way home from a conference in Miami. And I'm sitting next to my colleague Dennis, who's in first class because he screwed up — he took a job that requires him to fly across the country way too often.

Dennis is a rare find in the world of marketing — and not just because he likes me. It's because he has the fourth skill.

For a long time, there were two marketing "skills" — branding (although it was generally referred to more often as advertising) and direct marketing. I'm oversimplifying, of course, since within each of this disciplines there are a number of specialized (and no less important) skill sets.

Then along came the Internet, and a new skill family emerged — online marketing. This new skill family married technology, user interface design, and direct marketing skills.

How many marketers do you know can converse equally well with experts from all three disciplines?

I only know one: Dennis. He has the fourth skill. The fourth skill is the ability to help organizations create marketing strategies and plans that integrate the three disciplines. The ability to discuss marketing ROI with the financial folks as well as the marketers.

I don't think that at this point in his career that Dennis is looking to become a Chief Marketing Officer. Which is too bad, because he would be a good one. Successful CMOs in the future will need the fourth skill. Liking me is optional.

Chief Customer Experience Officer: A Bad Idea

I've recently seen calls for the creation of a Chief Customer Experience Officer (one from Forrester Research and one at E-Volve-or-Die.com).

This is a terrible idea. Why? Because creating a CCEO position:

- **Is superfluous.** Although the experts may have different definitions for what a "customer experience" is, I would hope that they would agree that it involves the interaction of a customer (or prospect) with a firm, its products, or marketing messages (print ad, web site, etc.). Many customer experience interactions are either demand cycle (including, but not limited to sales transactions) or customer service-related interactions. In most (if not all) medium- to large firms, there is already an executive in charge of the processes involved in providing these customer experiences.

- **Creates more problems than it solves.** What should the CCEO's budget be? Whose pocket is it coming out of? (Oh, I suppose your firm has a ton of excess funds just waiting for deployment). Who's going to report to the CCEO? Why? Why should the CCEO have a "seat at the table" (as some of the pundits have called for) and not somebody else not currently at the table?

I don't doubt that at many firms the so-called "customer experience" is lacking and that existing functional executives aren't customer-focused. But creating a new "chief" position doesn't fix the problem.

This isn't a new issue. In the late 90's it was the Chief Knowledge Officer that the pundits were crying out for, and in the early 90's, we heard the calls for the Chief Reengineering Czar. Few firms (outside of consulting firms) have these positions around today.

It's not that firms don't need to manage their knowledge, reengineer their processes, or create better customer experiences. It's that the way to do it is through cross-functional (or cross-LOB) project teams with the leadership and involvement of today's senior managers.

And it's time for the pundits to realize that simply creating a box on the org chart doesn't solve a firm's problems.

☺ The Hot New Profession: Consultainment

Tired of being a CMO or senior marketing executive? Don't want to be your firm's Chief Customer Experience Officer? There's a new path to fame and fortune in the age of mass confusion. Become a consultainer.

Want to break in to this hot new field? Here's the formula: Write a book, create a blog (or vice versa), then get hired to speak at conferences and company events.

Today's consultainers aren't strictly consultants (they don't do "projects" — the call to action on their blog is usually "hire me to speak!"). And they're not purely entertainers (like some comedians who make a good living speaking at corporate events).

A rare breed -- like Tom Peters and Seth Godin -- do both really well (actually, I take that back -- neither of them do much consulting). And few make the really big bucks. But the field is growing.

Better yet, the entries to barrier are low -- *real* low.

Did you know that (in the US, at least) you have to be certified to practice professions like law and medicine? It's true. And yet, apparently, anybody (and seemingly more and more bodies) can become a consultainer by claiming to be a management or marketing "thought leader."

A number of observers have astutely commented on the importance of thought leadership in a B2B marketing context. Jon Miller of Marketo advocates for using thought leadership to:

"…deepen your role as a trusted adviser, which in turn builds your brand and improves awareness. The goal is to stay within the buyer's awareness so that when she is ready to speak with a sales person, your company is an obvious choice."

But exactly what is thought leadership? And who qualifies to call himself a thought leader? In one marketing article I recently read the author's bio said that he is a "subject matter expert and thought leader in customer collaboration." Says who?

That's the problem. There's nobody to say so. And that's why I'm announcing the formation of the Institute of Thought leaders and Consultainment Hotshots (ITCH). To certify true thought leaders throughout the blogosphere.

Here's how it will work. Email me with your request to join. When I receive your email, the SCABs (Self-Certified Advisory Board members) will review your site's content to determine if you qualify.

This society (I guess I should call it a social network) will be a self-governing body, with a rotating advisory board. So while SCABs will come and go, the ITCH will always be there.

And remember — I'm not just the president of the club, I'm also a member.

Fixing The Marketing-CEO Disconnect

HBS Working Knowledge interviewed Harvard Business School professor Gail McGovern about fixing the disconnect between marketing and the CEO.[6]

McGovern: "Over the past 10 years the mix of marketing skills needed by a company has radically changed, and many senior execs…have not kept pace."

My take: This skill deficiency is a two-way street. For sure, non-marketing execs have lost touch with many areas of marketing expertise (but are experts in branding, of course). But on the other hand, few CMOs have the fourth skill crucial for CMO success.

McGovern: "While CEOs have commonly delegated advertising and advertising strategy to outside agencies, now they are delegating sales, distribution strategy, pricing, and product development to CMOs, who often lack overarching strategic responsibility."

My take: In which firms has the CEO delegated responsibility for sales, distribution strategy, and/or product development to the CMO? The problem is very much the opposite: The CMO should be involved with (not necessarily controlling) these functions, but isn't. Part of the issue here relates back to the point regarding skills. Many CMOs — overly focused on branding — haven't developed the skills required to participate in, let alone be responsible for, functions like distribution strategy and product development.

McGovern: "Boards and CEOs, have been lulled into complacency by CMOs."

My take: This comment came in response to a question about why marketing has evolved so far from the executive suite over the years. But it's hard to believe that this could be happening in that many companies to make this a valid statement. The issue lies with a firm's culture. Sales- and finance-driven cultures tend to marginalize marketing, or at the least, diminish its strategic importance in the firm. But it's not the CMO lulling the exec suite into complacency.

McGovern: "…[T]he yawning gap between actual revenue growth and investors' expectations is a ticking time bomb. Marketing is the way in which firms can close this gap because it encompasses all the activities of an organization that listen to the customers' voice and ultimately generates profitable relationships."

My take: Marketing does not "encompass all the activities…that listen to the customer." The voice of the customer is captured in areas like sales and customer service. The problem is that it isn't always shared beyond those departments. [And if that weren't bad enough, within marketing, the function that captures the voice of the customer (or tries to) — market research — isn't well integrated with other areas of marketing.] McGovern's statement is overly simplistic, it's symptomatic of the biggest problem CMOs already have — accountability without responsibility.

McGovern: "The key challenge [in aligning marketing activities with corporate strategy] is to develop a set of metrics that measure the impact of marketing activities against the goals of the corporation."

My take: Metrics are great — as a tool to manage marketing's operations, and to communicate its contributions and impact. But they're a risky way to achieve alignment. McGovern hints at this herself, with her example of Starbucks picking the wrong metric to link back to corporate strategy. How much time elapsed and pain did they experience before they figured that out? At a recent DMA Financial Services conference, Martha Rogers commented that it takes eight quarters to get Return On Customer (™ Peppers & Rogers) calculations right. That's a long time to not know if you're in alignment or not. The right metrics are critical for staying on track — but they're not the way to figure out which track to be on.

Overall, I'm somewhat surprised by Ms. McGovern's comments. Her executive credentials are impeccable. I'm left believing that this interview didn't quite capture her real-world experience and perspective.

What Marketers Should Learn From IT

It's not news that marketers are under the gun to demonstrate ROI. CIOs are laughing under their breaths — they've been dealing with this for 25 years.

And they've learned a few things about how to deal with the issue. (But they won't tell you, because, hey — misery loves company). If they did, they'd say:

1) **Lesson #1: Get your own house in order.** Successful CIOs learned quickly that no one on the management team wanted to hear about how data center issues or storage capacity troubles prevented them from focusing on end user apps. Picture an iceberg — smart CIOs kept internal issues below the waterline, and didn't let internal issues rise above the surface.

Marketing implication: Campaign performance or brand awareness metrics may be improving, if campaign execution is flawed, or reporting is slow because of data integration issues, marketing's credibility will continue to be questioned.

2) **Lesson #2: Be more transparent.** CIOs have tinkered with committees to prioritize IT opportunities, and relationship management positions to interact with other parts of the organization. Granted, some of these tactics worked better than others — but, where successful, they helped make IT more transparent to the rest of the firm. Prioritization was no longer a black box — and even if the ROI on IT was slow to improve, senior execs had better insights into why.

Marketing implication: CMOs striving to demonstrate (and improve) marketing's ROI can't turn the ship around in a quarter. But when requests for market share analyses, or the development of creative materials, disappear into the marketing black box, ROI improvement efforts will appear to be taking longer than they are.

3) **Lesson #3: Build strong relationships.** There's no silver bullet, but this is as close as it gets. When talking to successful CIOs about why IT was viewed as a strong contributor in their firm, many couldn't point to specific capabilities, practices, or processes. It was typically something less tangible — like the working relationships they had with execs and manager throughout the firm.

Marketing implication: As a marketing exec, *you* may know how critical relationships are, but what do your direct reports do to build relationships outside of marketing? The interpersonal relationships that marketing develops goes a long way towards informally improving the transparency described in lesson #2.

The "uber-lesson:" While marketing makes investments in [more or less] tangible capabilities like building brand awareness, analytics, and creative design, there are other — more intangible — things that it can do to improve its credibility and strategic impact.

What Finance Wants To Know From Marketing

A senior finance exec in a large organization told me:

"We know it's hard to calculate the ROI on all expenditures, and we're not looking for Marketing to do that. They have to invest in brand equity and market research and we don't expect them to link those investments directly to sales. That's not what we want from them."

Then what *does* finance want from marketing? CFOs want CMOs to answer questions about:

1. **Alignment.** How do you know you're making the right level of investment by LOB/product/market?

2. **Integration.** How are marketing efforts integrated across channels, media, and other marketing expenditures?

3. **Context.** How does marketing's results compare with how its performed in the past, and against our competition?

4. **Vision.** In which customers/markets/products should we invest our marketing dollars?

Simple questions with no easy answers. But marketers looking to raise marketing's profile within their firm should be able to:

- **Address them qualitatively.** Despite their own quantitative bent, smart financial execs know that marketing can't answer these questions to the 3rd decimal place. But they do want marketing to have defensible theories and explanations to address them.

- **Demonstrate a plan to answer them.** It's a dereliction of duty if marketing can't show what actions it plans to take over the next 12-24 months to fill in the gaps in their measurement knowledge. What models will marketing develop to help answer some of these questions? What competitive benchmarks are available?

Why Do You Segment Customers?

The marketing department at a large firm (with a strong sales-driven culture) was trying to get sales' support to launch a customer segmentation effort. In one meeting, the market research consultant presented her psychographic analysis of consumers, outlining seven segments. She recommended, based on the company's "brand positioning", that the firm disregard three of the segments and focus their advertising efforts on the other four.

At this point, one of the sales execs piped up and said "if the purpose of our segmentation effort is to exclude potentially profitable prospects, I can't support this." The project was dead in its tracks.

What mistake did marketing make? They didn't start by clearly defining — and communicating — WHY the firm needed a new customer segmentation approach. "Understanding differences in consumer behaviors and attitudes" isn't good enough. That's an academic exercise, few outside of marketing really care about. Successful segmentation efforts start with a definition of what the firm needs to do a better job of — e.g., targeting, offer development, product design — and how a customer segmentation scheme will help the company improve those areas.

What's Wrong With This Picture?

Forrester Research asked ~100 marketers which skills were most important to the success of a marketing executive, and how critical those skills are relative to five years ago.[7]

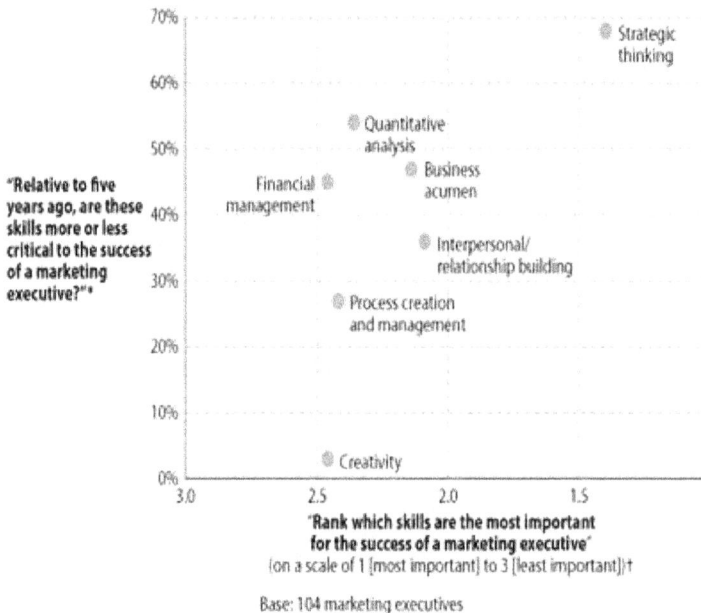

"Relative to five years ago, are these skills more or less critical to the success of a marketing executive?" *

Chart showing skills plotted:
- Strategic thinking (~68%, rank ~1.4)
- Quantitative analysis (~52%)
- Business acumen (~47%)
- Financial management (~44%)
- Interpersonal/relationship building (~35%)
- Process creation and management (~28%)
- Creativity (~2%)

'Rank which skills are the most important for the success of a marketing executive'
(on a scale of 1 [most important] to 3 [least important])†

Base: 104 marketing executives

Source: Forrester's Q2 2006 Marketing Organization Online Survey
*Net percentage calculated by subtracting the percentage of respondents who indicated 'more important today' from those who indicated 'less important today.'
†Ranks displayed are averages.

So what's wrong with this picture? The marketers got it completely wrong. The order should have been reversed.

Marketers earn the right to be "strategic" by the efficient and effective delivery of the processes they manage, and by demonstrating an ability to tie the results of their processes to the financial performance of their firm.

All too often, the word strategy is thrown around too casually. I bet the marketers surveyed by Forrester used the term "strategic thinking" to mean "large scale, disruptive, competitive-advantage gaining" thinking.

But often, strategy simply means "fix a problem" — which requires more creativity and process/financial management than it does pie-in-the-sky rumination.

Get your skill priorities straight, marketers.

Employee-Generated Strategy

Gene Blishen, General Manager of Mount Lehman Credit Union in British Columbia, Canada and blogger at Tinfoiling, wrote :[8]

"The lowest employee on the organization chart has the greatest contact with the customer. But why are they the least consulted when it comes to any change in process with the customer?"

My take: The reason is that there is a lingering perception among many senior execs that only they can (or should) set strategy.

A number of years ago, for a strategy consulting project I was leading (for a client we had already done work for), I put together a project plan that included interviews with a number of mid-level managers. My boss (the partner) asked me why I was planning to talk to "them," and I said it was because "they" knew what the real issues were — with the firm's customers, with the firm's capabilities, and with the firm's current strategy.

His response: "We're not going to talk to them. Only senior execs set strategy."

That was more than 10 years ago, and not a whole has changed. But it will.

While a lot of the discussion on the blogosphere and in the press focuses on the impact of social networking on the consumer landscape, less attention is being paid to how social networking — and the collaborative technologies that enable it — impact how we manage the organizations we work in.

Granted, there have been articles discussing the use of Wikis to enable team collaboration, but not a lot has been written about the impact on how corporate strategy is established.

One of the positive trends in the strategy thought-leadership world over the past few years has been the linkage of strategy to execution (e.g., Blue Ocean Strategy) and the need for organizational alignment regarding strategy (e.g., Alignment: Using The Balanced Scorecard To Create Corporate Synergies).

But most of the authors still start from a top-down perspective of how strategy is determined and decided upon. So we end up with recommendations to create "chief strategy officers" to monitor and align strategy development efforts — in effect (to create a visual), to manage the strategy waterfall.

This is going to change. Rather than create chief strategy officers — who serve as strategy state police, preserving the status quo, firms will change the way they formulate strategy in the first place. And "formulate" won't even be a word used in conjunction with strategy, because it has all the wrong connotations.

Michael Raynor gets this. In his book The Strategy Paradox, he recognizes that the focus and commitment required to generate the highest returns (the hallmark of today's strategy formulation approach) is in odds with an inherent inability to plan for an unknowable future. As a result, he advocates for the development of a new competency: "Managing strategic uncertainty through the creation of strategic options." As David Newkirk writes in Strategy-Business:

"As decisions move up the corporate hierarchy, executives' time horizons should lengthen and their priorities should shift from managing commitments to building options on an uncertain future. "CEOs should not see their role in terms of making strategic choices — that is, commitments," Raynor writes. "Rather, they should focus on building 'strategic options,'

that is, creating the ability to pursue alternative strategies that could be useful, depending on how key uncertainties are resolved."

As "decisions move up the corporate hierarchy"? Doesn't sound like a lot of today's firms, at least as it applies to strategic decisions.

Three factors are going to contribute to a new way of "doing" (avoiding that "formulating" word) strategy, which I think of as employee-generated strategy (think user-generated content, but much *much* better):

1) **Technology.** The tools are out there — blogs, Wikis, organizational visualization tools, etc. I'm not sure anyone has quite brought them together in a way to support a new way of doing strategy, though.

2) **Demographics.** If the younger generation (Gen Y, Millennials, or whatever you want to call them) are as collaborative as they claim to be, then they'll help bring about this change in strategy development.

3) **Experimentation.** Regardless of the technology or demographic factors, there's enough dissatisfaction out there to cause firms to experiment with how they develop strategy, and lead them to be more inclusive and collaborative with the process. And prove my old boss wrong — that is not only senior execs that set strategy.

☺ Translating CMO-Speak

The CMO Council always does a good job with its annual survey of marketing execs, and the 2008 report is no exception. Containing a lot of interesting findings.

While reading through them, though, I couldn't help but wonder if everyone understood what the execs surveyed were *really* saying. After all, they couch their true feelings in "CMO-speak." So allow me to translate this year's findings back into plain English:

Finding: 79% of execs surveyed believe marketing is making significant or reasonable progress improving the perceived value of the function.

Translation: "My mother thinks I'm doing a great job."

Finding: 50% of CMOs are hired to fix broken marketing organizations.

Translation: "The fact that I screwed things up so badly in my last job didn't deter my new firm from hiring me to fix what my predecessor screwed up."

Finding: 45% of marketers expect to change their agency.

Translation: "Told you it wasn't my fault things are screwed up."

Finding: 20% of marketers do not track and measure the return on their marketing spend.

Translation: "There's nothing to track."

Finding: The top two areas for marketing dollar allocation in 2008 are: 1) strategy and branding, and 2) events and trade shows.

Translation: "My wife likes to go to Las Vegas."

Finding: New competencies and capabilities are at the top of the list of organizational and operational changes planned for 2008.

Translation: "I have no idea what new competencies or capabilities I need to build, but I know that I need some new ones."

Finding: Peers are seen as the most trusted sources for marketing insight, information, and management practices.

Translation: "Misery loves company."

Finding: Blogs are the least influential source of marketing insight and management practices.

Translation: "I really don't care what you have to say, Shevlin."

SECTION 3: ROI MEASUREMENT AND REPORTING

The ROI On Brand Versus The Value Of Brand

The mechanics of measuring marketing ROI are well documented, and there are a lot of people out there who know a lot more about this topic than I do, and ever will.

But there's a lot of bad advice about this topic being spewed, and myths that need to be taken down. One of them is the supposed ROI on branding investments. A friend recently shared his views on branding:

"Clients often ask how to measure the ROI of branding efforts. Maybe the question needs to be redefined. Instead of "what is the ROI of brand," maybe it should be "what is the overall value of the brand?" Instead of asking, "How does brand create revenue?" ask, "How does brand contribute to my balance sheet?"

We intuitively know there's value in branding, but the bean counters want some dollar-for-dollar ratio on their investment — and I don't think it works like that.

Two firms of the same size could both spend $500k on branding but have radically different results. It hinges a lot on how they deliver the brand, the messages in their materials, the media they choose, the markets they serve, etc. But mostly, I'd say it hinges on how well they execute and deliver in first-hand interactions.

Many firms have the misconception that when they complete a branding project that the work is done. But it's like they have an infant that they will have to nurture with time, energy and money if they want to see it grow up to be a mature, responsible brand that makes positive contributions."

My take: My friend is on the right track by reframing the brand ROI question.

A brand is a lot like the servers in your data center. They're infrastructure — they're something you build applications upon. In and of themselves, they produce no return on their investment — you have to do something with them to generate a return.

It's the same with brand. Brand can create awareness, expectations, and even intention -- but it doesn't close the sale. Something (or things) else does that. Which means you can't calculate the ROI of brand. With carefully designed and executed tests, perhaps you could measure the contribution to sales that branding investments make, but few (if any) firms seem willing to take that route.

Over the past 20 years, CIOs have gotten a lot smarter about how to craft and justify their IT infrastructure investments. It took a lot of work on the part of the more successful CIOs to demonstrate how IT infrastructure enables and supports current and future business capabilities.

CMOs need to take a similar approach, and treat their investments in brand as infrastructure, and demonstrate how those investments enable the sales and marketing capabilities their firms develop. The free ride (i.e., spuriously linking brand investments to changes in sales) won't last forever.

The Cost Of Acquisition Versus The Cost Of Retention

How many times have you heard that it costs X times more to acquire a customer than to retain one? The most recent one for me was in an article in CRM magazine, in which the author wrote:

"According to Gartner it costs 8-10 times more to acquire customers that it does to retain them."

Oh really? I had heard it was five times more, but I guess that with inflation and all, it's now eight to ten. Yeah, right. It's time to eliminate this urban legend from our repertoire. Here are just a few of the reasons why the claim that acquisition is so much more costly than retention is pure fiction. The costs of acquisition and retention:

- **Vary by industry, by product, and company strategy.** Don't tell me that the ratio is eight or ten to one across every product and industry. The automotive industry probably has a fifty (or hundred) to one acquisition to retention ratio. Car dealers, as far as I can tell, don't spend a dime on customer retention. In the world of financial services, though, I'd bet that HSBC and Emigrant Savings have effectively acquired savings account customers online with above-average industry rates. Retaining — and, as importantly, cross-selling — those customers could not have been as easy.

- **Ebb and flow with economic cycles.** Lenders found it a whole lot cheaper to acquire new mortgage and home equity loan applicants a few years ago than they do today. And why would anybody assume that retaining those borrowers from a few years ago was a piece of cake that didn't require much investment? Hogwash.

- **Are incalculable.** You have no clue how much it costs to retain customers. Do you include all the costs associated with providing customer service to customers in your retention calculations? After all, if you don't service them, you will have less chance of retaining them. Do you allocate all IT application maintenance and enhancements to your retention calculations? If you don't continually improve your transaction and interaction service capabilities, your ability to retain customers diminishes, you know.

No, the fact of the matter is that you don't have the slightest clue what it costs to retain a customer, because no one has really defined a standard for what costs to include and which ones to exclude.

So the next time you find yourself wanting to cite the "fact" that the cost of acquiring customers is X times greater than the cost of keeping them, do us all a favor. Don't. Cuz' it ain't true.

Why Do Marketers Test?

Jim Novo, an interactive customer loyalty expert, and author of Drilling Down: Turning Customer Data Into Profits With A Spreadsheet, commented that few online marketers deploy testing the way it's often done in the offline world.[9] He speculates that the reasons for this include cultural issues and a lack of ideas about what meaningful tests to conduct. This raises a more fundamental question: Why do marketers test in the first place?

You could argue that the answer to that is simple — to increase the effectiveness of marketing programs. But there's another side of the coin: To improve the efficiency of marketing programs.

In the "old" world of direct marketing, where direct mail costs are significant, marketers test to determine who not to mail to. But in the online world, where the incremental cost of sending out one more email is practically non-existent, suppressing marketing messages is less of an issue.

So why should online marketers bother to test? If online marketing response rates are higher than direct mail response rates, and little opportunity to reduce campaign costs, then marketers will have little incentive to test.

The distinction — and balance — between effectiveness and efficiency is subtle. Marketers who recognize that their tests have been more focused on efficiency than effectiveness will realize that they're missing many opportunities to create and execute a strategic test and learn agenda that not improves effectiveness but drives marketing strategy.

The notion of a test and learn agenda isn't new. But many database marketers' test and learn agenda is undeveloped, underdeveloped, or misguided. Often, testing plans are focused on short-term and tactically-oriented questions like who should be mailed to, and which messages work better than others.

There's a bigger opportunity here, specifically, to test to help answer more strategic marketing questions like:

- What number of touches is best for which customer segments?

- How can a sequence of messages help lift response?

- How does time between touches effect response and conversion rates?

The opportunity to be more strategic with testing isn't limited to marketing effectiveness. In many firms, it falls on the shoulders of market research to answer questions about consumer behaviors and attitudes. But far too often, market research is burdened with addressing tactical issues. Database marketers can step in and help here, and devise tests to help understand:

- Which customer behaviors are most closely correlated with response and conversion and help define an "engaged" customer?

- What is the optimal spend per customer to increase customer engagement?

- What is the profit per customer impact of increased customer engagement?

Database marketers — or online marketers, for that matter — won't be able to answer these questions if their testing approaches are limited to figuring out who not to touch. Or if they don't test at all, for that matter. Marketing needs a new mindset about testing, and break out of the confines of campaign-centric ROI test and measurement.

Marketing's Key Performance Indicators

Gary Angel and Eric Peterson are web analytics experts with interesting views on web analytics KPIs. Eric says:[10]

"KPIs should be included or excluded from a hierarchical reporting strategy...based on the likelihood that the indicator will spur some type of action in the organization when the indicator unexpectedly changes...[although] the action the organization would take, when unexpected change occurs, is never precise."

Gary's take is more context-oriented:[11]

"A report becomes actionable by using KPIs to provide the business context within which an action can be identified or deemed worth trying. The more relevant context a report provides, the more likely it is to be actionable. KPIs are the context builders that make up our view of what's important and what isn't."

My take: Constructing the "right" set of KPIs is not an either/or decision between actionability and context. CMOs should look at their KPIs as a portfolio of measures, each of which should meet at least one of these criteria:

- **Explanatory ability.** Perhaps closest to Gary's description of context, does the KPI help explain why what happened happened? (sorry if you have to read that twice).

- **Predictive ability.** Does the KPI enhance the firm's ability to predict what will happen in the future?

- **Behavior change.** Does the act of measuring the KPI incent people to act or behave in a particular way (that management believes is desirable)?

When evaluating a set of potential KPIs, marketing execs need to put each metric up against these criteria and ask themselves (at least) two questions:

1) **Does this metric help us explain, predict, or change behavior?** If not, then that metric may not be a good candidate for the KPI list.

2) **Is the set of metrics balanced between the criteria? If** all of the proposed KPIs are explanatory, then it's likely that reports will be "rear-mirror" focused, leaving senior execs frustrated that Marketing isn't looking ahead.

What about metrics that simply describe what happened? I'm not saying don't measure them. But they don't qualify as a KPI. Too many marketing scorecards are just a laundry list of metrics that senior execs often get elsewhere. To be effective, reports have to add value to execs' understanding of the business by explaining, predicting or changing behavior.

CYA (Count Your Assets)

In the October 2004 issue of the Journal of Marketing, Roland Rust and colleagues wrote that:

"Marketers are under pressure to show how marketing investments add to shareholder value…[and] must identify the assets in which they invest and how those assets contribute to profits."

Marketing executives know this all too well. But, in practice, few marketing departments actually define, track, and measure the assets they produce. Often, marketers simply take business value measures like sales and divide it by the sum of all marketing expenditures.

But what about all the other things marketing does and produces? The market studies, media tests, account plans, merchandising materials, brochures, web pages managed, supplier relationships managed? These are marketing's assets. And while they may not have a direct impact on sales, over time marketing should (and must) correlate the assets they produce to the bottom line.

To help get your arms around the assets that marketing produces, group them into three categories:

- **Sales assets.** These assets — like banner ads, direct mail pieces, merchandising materials, sales brochures — help produce or facilitate a sale. You know a sales asset when you see one because it touches your end customer or a sales person who's making a sale.

- **Information assets.** Information assets — for example, market studies, media test, account plans — are intangible, information-based assets that directly touch end customers, but impact marketing decisions made throughout the firm. The objective of tracking these assets is to demonstrate the influence that marketing has on how the firm invests its marketing dollars.

- **Infrastructure assets.** These assets don't directly touch end customers or even marketing's internal constituents. They're the assets that let marketing produce information and sales assets — like agency hours managed, research vendors managed, and media suppliers managed.

For each of the assets that your marketing department defines, you should track the hours and dollars spent producing those assets, and the business unit, product, and geographic market they're intended to support (which is why you'll need to be judicious in your choice of which assets to measure and track).

Defining and tracking marketing's assets gives CMOs the ability to show:

- What marketing produces with the firm's investment (which LOBs, products, geographies are getting their fair share — or more or less of their fair share — of investment?);

- Spending patterns over time (is the firm investing more or less in one type of asset vs. another over time); and

- The efficiency with which marketing produces its assets (are unit costs rising or declining over time? are infrastructure asset costs, as a percent of the total, increasing or declining over time?)

The Art And Science Of Marketing Scorecards

There are a lot of good articles about marketing scorecards. I'm not sure too many CMOs have read any of it, however. Too many marketing scorecards are overloaded with historical sales and marketing statistics, presented in mind-numbing detail.

Effective marketing scorecards strike a balance between measuring marketing ROI (the science) and reporting ROI (the art). Smart CMOs recognize that one piece of the marketing ROI puzzle is psychological — making other execs feel comfortable about how and where marketing dollars are being spent.

Reporting marketing ROI isn't a "fill-in-the-blanks of the template" exercise (which too many scorecards appear to follow). Effective scorecards tell a story. While there's no template, there are common elements (chapters) in good marketing ROI stories:

- **Spending.** Where did the money go? Marketing scorecards should show senior execs where the firm's marketing investment went. What products did we invest in? Which markets? Which LOBs? Which customer segments? What did we produce (i.e., marketing assets) with the marketing dollars we spent? How much did we spend on lead generation vs. brand equity vs. marketing productivity?

- **Results.** What did the spending get us? CMOs shouldn't confuse marketing ROI reporting with sales reporting. Marketing scorecards shouldn't be detailed reports of sales by LOB, geography, etc. This chapter is the flip side of chapter one — what are the trends in brand equity, lead gen, sales, and operational effectiveness.

- **Context.** This is where the story transitions from science to art. Why did what happened happen? How did we do against expectations — i.e., budgets, targets, and the rest of the industry? With which customer segments did we achieve better (or worse) than expected results? How did the investments we made last year (and the year before that) impact last quarter's results? How is the channel mix changing and what does this mean to our business? What adjustments in marketing investments do we need to make going forward?

Above all, effective marketing scorecards are documents of influence. They don't just tell what happened — they tell why and what it means. (And they don't take 40+ pages to do it).

Influence -- Don't Educate

A lot of conference presentations suck. There are a lot of reasons why, but one in particular is that too many presenters assume the role of educator.

Not a lot of presenters are even aware that their style and content have an educational tone to them. Their presentations are oriented towards answering the question: What can I tell you about what I know?

This isn't inherently bad or wrong. But it presumes that the:

1) Audience doesn't already know the topic. I see this a lot with Web 2.0 presentations. Seems like a lot of speakers want to educate the audience on "what" Web 2.0 is. But is that really the question the audience wants answered? Or would they rather like to know when to use Web 2.0 technology and when not to use it?

2) Presentation jives with audience's preferred style of learning. Even if the audience wants to be educated, is a Powerpoint presentation the most effective way for a majority of the audience to learn about it? Some people might learn about the topic more effectively through a hands-on demonstration.

3) Speaker is an effective educator. Not every presenter's style is well suited to playing the educator, though.

I know mine isn't. I always dread it when a client says "we need you to come in and educate us on [insert topic here]." I don't like playing the educator — I like playing the influencer. I want to get up there and tell the audience why they should be doing what I think they should be doing, or seeing the world the way I see the world.

With so many speakers playing the educator role, conferences can become redundant, repetitive, and downright boring.

What does this have to do with marketing? When reporting to senior management, Marketing often assumes the role of educator and not influencer.

I see a lot of reports that marketing sends to senior management. At the risk of insulting someone (i.e., a client), many marketers seem obsessed with pretty graphics and reams of data.

When I get a chance to evaluate a marketing report, I'll point to a specific slide or graph and ask "why is this slide in the deck?" The response I usually get is "management needs to know that." That answer isn't sufficient.

Marketing needs to evaluate each slide, graphic, or data point in their reports and ask themselves the questions: 1) Why are we putting this in the deck? and 2) What do we want management to do with it?

Not every page of the report has to lead to a specific action. It's OK if the answer to the questions is "we want management to see that we were successful and want to continue the course." But that's still influence-based reporting, and not education. It's influencing senior exec's perceptions of what's working or not working with marketing's investments.

Another comment I'll often get is "management asked for this data." Yes, they did. A year ago. When the crisis du jour was understanding why sales in the midwest territory was declining. But what happens with marketing reports? Once in, never out.

For sure, marketing reports need to address "what it is." But to be effective, marketing needs to address "what it means." And focus on influencing, and not just educating.

Hiding Behind The Veil Of Experimentation

As the early Baby Boomers (or should I just say people born between 1945 and 1955) come of presidential age, we're sure to hear more politicians admit to having "experimented" with marijuana in their college days.

As if experimenting makes that OK. Is it OK to experiment with grand theft auto? How about experimenting with treason? OK, fine, those aren't fair comparisons. And my point here isn't political, but marketing-related.

My take: Too many marketers (online marketers, in particular) are deploying questionable tactics, hiding behind a veil of "experimentation." Example: User-generated content (UGC) campaigns.

I don't doubt that a large bank that's currently running a UGC campaign will succeed in pulling in a thousand, if not a couple of thousand, entries. But I can't help but wonder if they've established targets for and are measuring:

- The mix of entries from prospects and existing customers
- How many prospects are converted to customers
- The up-sell/cross-sell success for customers who submit entries

And I also wonder what marketing would say if the CEO or CFO asked: What other potential initiatives — which were not funded — were deemed less important than this one, and why?

A marketing exec at the bank said (on a blog) "this is a test, so we're not certain either how it will turn out, but we feel it's worth a try."

Worth a try based on what? A desire to be one of the cool kids? To be able to say "we're a cool brand because we did a UGC campaign"?

It isn't only the lack of economic rationale that's bothering me here, but a more fundamental issue which is prevalent in all-too-many marketing departments: The absence of a rigorous test-and-learn discipline.

I'm all for experimenting (in a marketing context, that is). But a marketing group that creates a disciplined test-and-learn agenda establishes key questions that it wants to find the answers to.

Understanding whether or not consumers who submit entries into a UGC contest are good (better?) candidates for acquisition/cross-sell may very well be a valid question. But I'm willing to bet that: 1) most firms have more burning questions to address, and 2) the bank in question did not establish this question as part of a test-and-learn agenda.

Experimentation is not a way out of accountability. And considering the accountability issues that so many marketing groups face today, hiding behind a veil of experimentation doesn't make things better.

☺ Books That Seth Godin Should Have Written

Having read the pile of books I took out of the library, I broke down and started reading Seth Godin's book The Dip, which I got for free at a conference. After page three, I had had enough, and started thinking about the books that Godin should have written:

- The Dip Shit: A Little Book That Teaches You How To Deal With Lousy Bosses

- Purple Haze: Transform Your Business By Doing LSD

- The Big Yoo: Stop Trying To Be Perfect And Start Accepting Your Weight Problem

- The Big Dead Prez: How To Make Any Democrat Feel Better

- Small Is The New Big: The Power Of Telling Authentic Lies To Dumb-Ass Consumers

- The Bootlicker's Bible: There's never been a better time to kiss the boss' ass. This manifesto will show you how.

Now those are books I might get past page three on.

SECTION 4: CUSTOMER EXPERIENCE MANAGEMENT

The Future Of Customer Experience Management

Christopher Meyer and Andre Schwager's February 2007 Harvard Business Review article "Understanding Customer Experience" brings, perhaps for the first time, the topic of customer experience management (CEM) to the senior management plane.[12] While the article is quite good, one thing stuck out like a sore thumb — the authors' definition of the term:

"[CEM] captures and distributes what a customer thinks about a company."

We used to call that market research.

But I don't want to argue about the definition. Instead, I see this definition as a milestone and as a potential turning point customer experience management's evolution.

In their 1994 book Beyond The Hype, three Harvard b-school professors postulated that the strength — and weakness — of many management techniques was that they could be defined in different ways to suit different purposes. Case in point #1: Reengineering, which was originally conceived as the redesign of cross-functional business processes and later, as it become more ingrained (and infamous), as synonymous with layoffs and downsizing. Later on in the 90s, knowledge management similarly meant many different things to different people.

From my perspective, management concepts go through a predictable cycle of four stages. They: 1) begin to dot the management press with articles from early proponents; 2) gain strong acceptance when credible case studies highlight the superior performance firms realize from deploying the concept; 3) fall out of favor as copycat firms begin to over-use the label and apply it to initiatives that shouldn't be funded (but get funded anyway because they have the label); and then 4) become part of the fabric of management if — and only if — they're truly a worthwhile management concept.

When CEM first started appearing as a term a few years ago, I thought it was the perfect antidote to reengineering. Whereas reengineering was about process redesign from the firm's POV (reduce cost and cycle time), I thought CEM would evolve to be about process redesign from the customer's POV (reduce cycle time IF it resulted in higher satisfaction, add cost IF it resulted in higher satisfaction).

But that hasn't really happened. David Raab recently commented on the variations of CEM frameworks, and the inherent differences they wrestle with regarding function vs. emotion, moments-of-truth vs. all experiences, static vs. interactive experiences, and expected vs. actual experiences.[13] In many firms, the term customer experience has been hijacked by the Web site designers and applies only to customers' online experiences.

So whither CEM?

CEM has labored in stage one for a while now. But whereas Michael Hammer's HBR article from long ago helped kick reengineering into stage two, I doubt that Meyer and Schwager's article will do the same. It failed to pull together the conflicting perspectives of the CEM frameworks that are out there, and, just as importantly (if not more so) it failed to provide the high-profile (and credible) case studies that demonstrate the radical and/or transformational impact CEM might have on a firm.

The heydays of management techniques like reengineering, knowledge management, or CEM don't last forever — they get anywhere from two to five years to gain acceptance, and if worthy, become part of how future managers run their organizations.

Customer experience management is probably in the middle of that lifecycle. If proponents don't come together to reconcile the conflicts in their frameworks and provide credible high-profile case studies that capture the attention of senior execs — before the end of 2008 — then CEM won't be a term we'll hear a lot about come 2010.

The Importance Of Cross-Channel Customer Experience Design

Blogger Alain Jourdier, at Marketing Bytes Man, tells of his bad experience opening a bank account online:[14]

I recently opened an account online and then the next day went to the branch and deposited cash into the account. After a few days, I paid a credit card bill online using this account. I was surprised when I got an email from the credit card company alerting me that they hadn't received the payment. The bank told me that all account balances opened online are held for 30 days! That's why they rejected the payment even though I had put cash in the account. I repaid it again from the same account after a supervisor told me that it would go through, [even though] their call center told me there was a hold on the account. I paid the credit card company with another account….and rode down to the branch and closed the account. The branch folks insisted the money was there and that there was no hold and could I please give them a chance to rectify it. But after two days of hassles and time lost….no way."

My take: There are important lessons about customer experience to learn from Alain's travails:

1) Customer experience is inseparable from business process. Smart marketers spend less time and money on branding efforts, and more on process quality and integration. Banks have enabled customers to open accounts online for years now. But few (and clearly not the one in Alain's story) have redesigned the account opening process from a cross-channel perspective.

Instead, the focus is on site design and the online account opening process. My bet is that site design was not a factor in winning Alain as a customer (that is, he made his decision to apply because of the checking account's features, and applied online because it was the most convenient way to do so). But poor process design was a major contributor in losing Alain as a customer.

2) Customers' expectations are an integral part of process design. It's understandable (if you're in the industry) why the bank put a hold on the account. Understandable — but not defensible. If Alain already had other accounts at the bank in question, then the hold is inexcusable.

Even more inexcusable, however, is that the bank didn't understand that Alain (like many other online consumers) expected the funds to be available immediately. Maybe there was notification of a hold on the bank's site, and Alain just missed it. It's still the bank's fault for not understanding the expectation and ensuring that its customer was aware of the hold.

3) Boring trumps WOW. The scary part of this example is that you never know where the stories that customers tell themselves are going to come from. Branch personnel did everything one could have expected them to — they were courteous, helpful, vowed to rectify the issue, etc.

But the story Alain has etched in his mind is "I opened an account, put money in, and they told me it wasn't there". If the bank could have simply understood his expectations — and delivered on it — then it would still have a customer, and the story Alain tells might be "I couldn't believe it — I opened the account, and started writing checks against it within the hour. Amazing."

WOW: Way Over wRated

On my Marketing Whims blog, a visitor commented:[15]

"Loyalty economics is not the study of "satisfying" my needs. That's been the problem with banking. Our goal has been to satisfy. We're running an errand. What are my expectations? Get in. Get out. Nobody gets hurt. I would say my bank meets those. Ken Blanchard said it best in his book Raving Fans: "Your customers are only satisfied because their expectations are so low, and because nobody else is doing any better." If you WOW me I will recommend you to my friends. That's the ONLY marketing that works today. Period. If you meet my expectations I probably won't say anything bad (or good) about you."

My take: While WOW is an admirable goal, not only is it NOT the "only marketing that works", it's not marketing at all. WOW:

- **Doesn't scale.** The problem with many great customer service stories floating around the blogosphere is that they're isolated examples. They're stories of heroic -- not institutionalized -- experiences. They don't scale. I can only imagine that marketers will read the comment quoted above, and ask "how do I build 'wow' into my direct mail and email campaigns?" or "how can I wow someone on every Web site visit?" The answer: They can't.

- **Isn't measurable.** One man's WOW is another man's yawn. To institutionalize WOW, you have to know what wows people. But can you imagine asking customers "what wows you?" I can't. The flip side to this is measuring a firm's ability to provide WOW. If cycle time, error rate, and throughput measures don't capture WOW, then what does? The answer: Nothing does.

Marketing is (or strives to be) a management discipline that is built on scalable, measurable, and repeatable processes and concepts. WOW is a bromide. It makes for great stories, helps Blanchard and

Peters sell books, but is far from being a platform around which a firm builds its marketing programs.

When I talk about customers' expectations, I'm referring to their expectations about the kind of relationship they want to have with the bank or credit union — not simply their expectations about individual transactions or interactions.

This is what's missing in many financial firms' marketing approach. Customers don't just differ in their product needs, buying behaviors, and psychographic dimensions. Different customers want different kinds of relationships.

I often wonder if my bank thinks it's "wowing" me when my designated account manager calls me every three months to ask "how's it going?" The bank might think that wows me because no other bank in the area does that.

But it doesn't WOW me — in fact, it ticks me off. It's a waste of my time.

The bank doesn't understand that I don't want to grow my relationship with it. Why? It's made too many transactional errors in the past — and therefore, I won't trust it with the big bucks. Operational excellence is what I expect (and value), and it's a necessary condition for growing the relationship. Other customers want (expect, value) different things, like unbiased guidance and advice regarding their financial decisions. That's the precondition they have to growing their relationship with their bank.

If you don't understand these "expectations" — and how they differ across customers — then you can NOT be a successful marketer.

If my bank wants to grow its relationship with me, it has to start with an understanding of these expectations. It has to either better deliver on the things I value or get me to change what I value that's aligned with what the bank does well. Simply calling me every quarter and asking me how it's going won't change that. Nor will misguided attempts to WOW me.

But will I tell my bank that I'll refer them to my friends and family? Sure. Because if I say no, somebody's bound to call me and waste my time trying to find out why not.

Quien Es Mas Stupido?

Remember when Saturday Night Live used to play Quien Es Mas Macho? I'm going to play Quien Es Mas Stupido? Here are today's contestants:

Contestant #1 is my Internet services provider. I agreed to upgrade to their fiber optic service and made an appointment to have a technician install the service. But when my wife explained to me that they were simply promising to send somebody out between 8AM and noon — and not complete the service within that window (tack on another 4-6 hours for the actual work to get done) — I called and canceled the upgrade.

But at the originally scheduled time, guess who shows up? My wife tells the guy we canceled, and calls me at work. I call the company, and they confirm that yes, I did indeed call and cancel.

Three days later, another technician shows up and starts spray-painting the lawn (maybe he's marking his territory to keep the gas company guy away). My wife again tells him we canceled and calls me at work. I call the company and ask if they have a record of my cancellation AND an entry for the call I placed three days earlier. The rep says "yes, I see both calls in the system. Let me get a supervisor."

The supervisor gets on and says "OK, I see the problem here. When you originally called to cancel the service, the order was canceled, but not the service appointment." Me: "Call me crazy, but it seems to me that when a customer cancels a service, the installation appointment should be automatically canceled." Supervisor: "That's a great idea — I'll pass it along."

Contestant #2 is a restaurant, part of a national chain. The other night, at 5PM, I called and made a reservation for 5:45 that evening. When we got there, we were handed a square vibrator and told it would be a 10-15 minute wait — even though the restaurant was only half full. When I asked why, I was told they were "short-staffed." But there were — no exaggeration — FIVE hosts/hostesses standing around the check-in desk AND two more holding the doors open (not that anybody was actually coming in, mind you).

The manager came to the front after a few minutes, and I asked him why, with all the empty tables AND a reservation we had to wait. He apologized, and again gave me the "short staffed" explanation. I said "you know — if it were MY restaurant, I'd take 4 or 5 of the SEVEN people standing around doing nothing, and give them a pencil and piece of paper, teach them to say What Would You Like?, and send them out throughout the restaurant. But hey, who am I to tell you how to run your business?"

So…. Quien Es Mas Stupido?

The answer, of course, is ME. I'm El Stupido. For expecting better. And for thinking I can change the minds of the WOW groupies and Chief Customer Experience Officer believers who think stuff like that matters. It doesn't. If you got things right the first time (and not even every time — 95% of the time would do) — you'd already be providing a differentiating customer experience.

☺ Marketing Math 101

A study by Marketing Management Analytics found that just 7% of senior financial execs were satisfied with their company's ability to measure marketing ROI.

Is it any wonder, considering:

- The CMO Council reports "the majority of marketers feel that their top goal is to quantify and measure the value of marketing programs and investments." A "majority" of 44%, that is.

- Chief Marketer publishes an article about winning marketing awards that tells readers that 1% of the entries come in in the first weeks, 65% on the day of the deadline, and 44% the day after the deadline. If only my employer gave me 110% of my salary every pay check.

Granted, some of the dissatisfaction on the part of the financial folks stems from their self-perception as the gurus of measurement. But they have an unfair advantage: They use calculators.

SECTION 5: CUSTOMER ENGAGEMENT

Customer Engagement Is Measurable

Avinash Kaushik is the author of one of the leading books in Web analytics space, "Web Analytics: An Hour A Day." On his popular Occam's Razor blog, he claims that engagement is not a metric:[16]

"Engagement is not a metric that anyone understands and even when used it rarely drives the action/improvement on the website....It is nearly impossible to define engagement in a standard way that can be applied across the board."

My take: This is too narrow a view of the term engagement, and the ability to measure it.

The biggest issue with the way the term engagement is used in the marketing community is its narrow connection to websites and the online channel. When marketers think of "customer engagement", they should be thinking about how engaged the customer is with the company, product, or brand. The level of involvement with the website — or with a particular ad (online or offline) — is just one dimension of a customer's engagement.

Customer engagement encompasses a number of dimensions:

1. Product involvement. A customer who doesn't care about the product, is likely to be less committed or emotionally attached to the firm providing the product.

2. Frequency of purchase. A customer who purchases more frequently may be more engaged than other customers.

3. Frequency of service interactions. Branding experts like to say that repeated, positive interactions lead to brand affinity. And they're right to a certain extent, but....

4. Types of interactions. …not all types of interactions are created equally. Checking account balances is a very different type of interaction than a request to help choose between product or service options.

5. Online behavior. Time spent on a site might be very important. But, like types of interactions, not all web pages are created equally.

6. Referral behavior/intention. Customers who are likely to refer a firm to friends/family might be more engaged — a customer who actually does refer the firm, even more engaged.

7. Velocity. The rate of change in the above indicators may signal engagement.

Avinash is on the right track, however, when he says that it's nearly impossible to define engagement in a standard way. I believe that a standard definition is feasible -- but that measuring it in a universally standard way is what's impossible. And that's good.

Who said we need a standard way of measuring engagement? The insistence on a standard definition and approach is silly. You don't hear anyone getting all worked up about the fact that market share can be calculated any number of ways, and that the denominator in that metric isn't consistent or easily measured.

Measuring engagement needs to be done in the context of a firm's strategy and it's own theory of the customer — that is, what behaviors the firm believes constitutes an engaged customer.

Measured correctly, engagement meets one of Avinash's golden rules — to be instantly useful. Using market research data, I measured customers' engagement with their banks using the attributes described above.

Customer Engagement

	Low	High	
High[1]	11%	11%	% of customers
	53%	53%	Very satisfied
Breadth of	46%	46%	Purchase intent[3]
relationship	11%	11%	% of customers
Low[2]	53%	53%	Very satisfied
	46%	46%	Purchase intent

[1] Owns 3 or more products with bank
[2] Owns 2 or less products with bank
[3] Intends to purchase more products at bank in next 12 months

I segmented respondents into four categories, based on their level of engagement, and the breadth of their relationship with their banks (based on the number of products owned). The impact of increased customer engagement: Increased purchase intention. Engaged customers are twice as likely to purchase more products than customers who aren't (see graphic above).

Marketers need to stop getting their knickers in a knot trying to boil engagement down to a single metric that relates to a web site or the online channel. It's a descriptor of a customer's attitudes, not a channel's performance.

A metric, when used appropriately, can help execs make decisions and manage. But considering the way engagement is being defined and measured today, it's no wonder Avinash has come to the conclusions that he has.

Stop Investing In Customer Retention

Target Marketing reported that marketers plan to shift media budgets from customer acquisition to retention.[17] If this is true for banks, it's troubling because:

- **Media spending isn't going to impact banks' retention rates.** Many banks report 15% to 20% annual account attrition. Yet the percentage of consumers who intend to switch banks, by closing out accounts, is in the low single digits. Why? People move, get married, get new jobs — and, banks screw up from time to time. No amount of media spend is going to fix that.

- **What it's really alluding to is cross-selling existing customers.** But many of these efforts are doomed to fail as well.

Many bank marketers cite BAI research that showed that bank customers were most likely to purchase additional products from their bank within six months of opening their initial account. If that's true, then pushing more products to the majority of customers with more than a year of tenure with the bank is destined to produce a disappointing ROI.

So what should marketers do? Invest in customer engagement. Many marketers think it's a buzzword. But it's a valid concept if used it to describe the extent to which your customers interact with you in meaningful, emotional ways. Not just by checking their balances, but by relying on you for advice and guidance on how to manage their financial lives and make smart financial decisions.

While the ROI may not be immediate, an investment in engagement is better than an investment in retention. The key to future profitability isn't in simply keeping customers — it's from deepening their relationships. And engagement is a necessary pre-condition for that to happen.

In addition, marketers get a metric that is immediately useful in helping them address strategic questions (see graphic below).

Measuring engagement helps marketers answer...

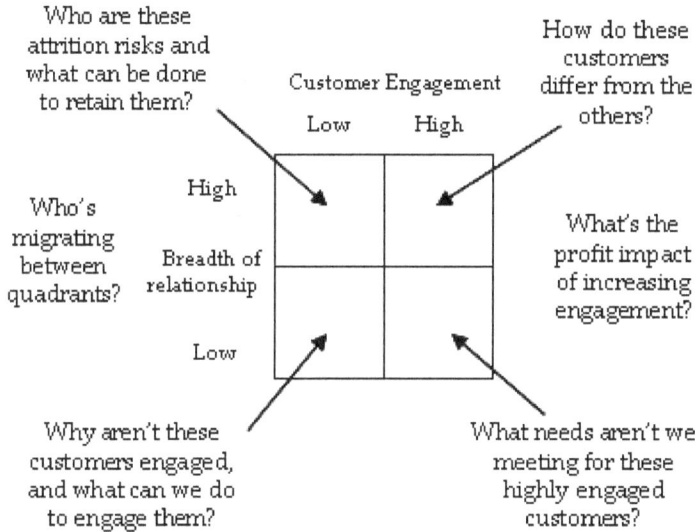

Who are these attrition risks and what can be done to retain them?

How do these customers differ from the others?

Customer Engagement

Low   High

Who's migrating between quadrants?

High

Breadth of relationship

Low

What's the profit impact of increasing engagement?

Why aren't these customers engaged, and what can we do to engage them?

What needs aren't we meeting for these highly engaged customers?

Denigrating Customer Engagement

An article in Ad Age claimed that:[18]

New research from Omnicom Group's OMD may move the seemingly fuzzy concept of engagement beyond the realm of academic debate by proving it really does move sales. The research indicated that not only does consumer engagement with media and advertising drive sales, but it also can drive sales more than media spending levels."

The study, which covered three unnamed financial services brands, found three drivers of consumer brand preference: 1) how engaged consumers were with the ad itself, with a weighting of 49%; 2) how engaged consumers were with the media where the ad appeared, weighted at 31%; and 3) how much consumers like the brand at the outset, with a 20% weighting.

My take: The problem with these conclusions start at the beginning — with the definition of customer engagement as time spent viewing an ad. I propose this definition of customer engagement:

"Repeated — and satisfying — interactions that strengthen the emotional connection a consumer has with a brand (or product, or company)."

According to Wikipedia, this definition "has gained currency and was used in the first international Annual Online Customer Engagement Survey", conducted by British consultancy cScape (which built upon, and improved, my definition).

But OMD (and, for the most part, the rest of the advertising industry) ignores this definition. It reduces the concept of engagement to the level of interaction a consumer has with an ad, and then equates time spent viewing an ad with driving "brand preference." These findings are hard to swallow. They ignore:

1) Customer experiences. The extent to which consumer experiences — sales experiences, support and service experiences, and experiences using the product or service — impact brand preference is either completely ignored or buried in the concept of "how much a consumer likes the brand at the outset" before viewing an ad.

2) Direct marketing. Financial services marketers are active direct marketers, extensively using direct mail and email. How OMD can tie ad "engagement" directly to sales, without incorporating the impact of these other marketing channels, was not explained. Increasingly, financial services marketers are adopting net measurement techniques, and developing uplift models to predict and measure the incremental impact of specific marketing actions. Yet OMD apparently has no problem directly attributing sales to time spent viewing ads, without factoring in the impact of other influences.

3) Sales effectiveness. If the OMD study had linked its measure of engagement to brand affinity, I might not have such an issue with it. But taking the impact to ROI (i.e., a sale), the study ignores the fact that many financial product sales are intermediated by a sales person. An ad may drive response, but to simply assume that that response produces a sale is wrong. Many a bank branch or mortgage rep has blown a sale due to poor salesmanship.

The question the study attempts to answer — "what impact does ad viewing have on sales?" — is simply not an answerable question.

The questions that need to be answered are "how do consumers buy?" and "what is the appropriate role and impact of various media and touchpoints in the consumer's decision process?"

To address these questions, financial services marketers need a "theory of the customer" that defines the kinds of relationships they want, what does it mean to be engaged given different types of relationships, and how to measure and drive those forms of engagement. Reducing the concept of customer engagement down to "time spent viewing an ad" denigrates a potentially important strategic concept.

Unfortunately, marketers looking for help in addressing these issues are going to have to wait while the advertising industry plays its "my metric is better than your metric" games.

Customer Engagement: The Agency/Client Perception Gap

cScape's second annual Customer Engagement (CE) survey reveals some interesting gaps in perceptions between agency and client-side respondents.[19] These differences in perception show up in questions about:

- **The importance of customer engagement.** Only 35% of agency respondents said that online customer engagement is essential to their clients, in contrast to half of client-side respondents. Both groups were aligned, though, in their perception of increasing importance of the concept: About 75% of both groups said that customer engagement had increased in importance to clients over the past 12 months.

- **The impact of customer engagement initiatives.** Compared to client-side respondents, agency respondents were more likely to say that CE initiatives improved their clients' customer loyalty and increased revenue. In fact, twice as many agency respondents said that CE initiatives increased profits than client-side respondents did.

- **What clients use to increase online customer engagement.** Forty-one percent of agency respondents think that their clients use blogging sites to increase engagement, but just 19% of clients said that they use these sites. This discrepancy carried over to the use of social networks, video-sharing sites, and image-sharing sites (e.g., Flickr).

- **The future role of the mobile channel.** Almost one-third of the agency respondents said that the mobile channel will be essential for customer engagement in the next three years. Just 20% of client-side respondents shared that view, though.

- **The description of an engaged customer.** Both groups agree that an engaged customer recommends the product, service, or brand. But the two groups differ in their view to the extent that an engaged customer purchases regularly. Clients were more likely to believe this than agency respondents.

- **How customer engagement is measured.** Nearly one-half (49% to be exact) of client-side respondents said that their firm has dedicated metrics for measuring online customer engagement. But just 30% of the agency respondents said that their clients have dedicated metrics.

- **The barriers to cultivating better online engagement.** Client-side respondents were half as likely as agency respondents to believe that their own lack of skills and experience are a barrier to better CE. The two groups' views also diverged regarding the extent to which getting senior management buy-in, dealing with technology problems, and finding supporting agencies were a barrier.

It's highly unlikely, of course, that the client-side respondents were clients of the agency respondents. But the discrepancies in responses can't help but make me wonder if many agency people aren't on the same page with their clients when it comes to customer engagement. A number of factors are driving this discrepancy, specifically the agencies':

1) Tendency to overstate impact. Often, the agencies aren't the ones measuring the results, so I'm not sure why they'd think that customer engagement efforts are having such a great impact. Or why any of the branding campaigns they're involved are having such a great impact, for that matter. But, hey, they're not going to say that their efforts didn't pay off, are they?

2) Over-fascination with the new. The client-side people are in the trenches fighting daily battles and fires. Few have time to explore video- and image-sharing sites or to read (and write) blogs. The agency-side, however, with a broader perspective, is out there looking for the next new big thing. So they attribute the involvement they do see out there to a wider range of client-side firms than are actually participating in these sites.

3) Mismatch of definition. A lot of the agency-side discussion of customer engagement has revolved around the concept as a measure of media effectiveness. A lot of marketers on the client-side don't care about that. They're looking at customer engagement as a potential way to help them make smarter decisions about investing their marketing dollars, and for helping them gauge their success.

☺ Other Uses For Personalized Billboards

News of the personalized billboards (that display a personalized message on a billboard as you drive by) that Mini Cooper is testing got me thinking of some other firms that might use this new medium:

- Ron Shevlin, your current bank balance is $1.17.
  Get a payday loan at Sonic Cash.

- Ron Shevlin, your STD tests are in, contact us immediately.
  Lahey Clinic

- Thank you for your continued business, Ron Shevlin.
  From your friends at Frenchy's Adult Book Store.

- The air in your front left tire looks low, Ron Shevlin.
  Lou's Mobil station (one block ahead).

- Ron Shevlin: Your alimony payment is three months late.
  Massachusetts Association of Divorce Lawyers.

- Ron Shevlin: Your alimony payment isn't the only thing that's late.
  American College of Obstetricians and Gynecologists.

- Only wimps drive a Mini Cooper, Ron Shevlin.
  Land Rover of Peabody.

On second thought, maybe personalized billboards aren't such a good idea.

SECTION 6: CUSTOMER LIFETIME VALUE

How Do You Measure Customer Lifetime Value?

In the October 2007 issue of Harvard Business Review, an article titled How Valuable Is Word Of Mouth discusses the distinction between customers' lifetime value (CLV) and referral value.[20] The article says this about CLV:

"Estimating a CLV is relatively straightforward. The value to FirmCo of all that Mary will ever buy equals the amount that her purchases will contribute to FirmCo's operating margin minus the costs of marketing to her."

Oh really? And what should we do with the costs of providing service to Mary during her tenure as a customer? Ignore them? Assume they're equal across customers?

The article goes on to say:

"No one really knows how much Mary will buy from FirmCo in the future, but we can make an estimate by analyzing her past purchases over some period of time…then projecting that pattern forward using sophisticated statistical models."

This is a fairly common practice in many firms. This approach ignores two important factors, however:

1) Life stage events. In research I did that looked at the impact of moving on consumers' purchase habits, I found — not surprisingly — that consumers who move make a lot of purchases in and around the time of their move. But, more interestingly, many consumers change their ongoing purchase habits — sometimes spending more, sometimes spending less — in many product/service categories, depending on the reasons for the move. Most CLV calculations, even those employing "sophisticated" models, miss these events.

2) Moments of truth. A term coined by McKinsey, these customer interactions leave an indelible mark on the relationship. If positive, they can amplify the relationship — if negative, they could kill it altogether. I'm not aware of any firm that explicitly incorporates the possibility or likelihood of these "relationship disrupters" in their CLV calculations.

The HBR article makes a case for why — and how — to incorporate referral value into a CLV calculation. But marketers should also: 1) incorporate service costs; 2) account for life stage events; and 3) model for relationship disrupters.

Further Thoughts On Customer Lifetime Value

In measuring or modeling customer lifetime value, marketers need to:

1) Incorporate measures of risk. CLV boils down to a single number. But there are a number of variables and assumptions that feed that number — variables whose values: a) are estimated at the time of calculation, and b) change over time.

Channel behavior is a good example of this. In banking, a customer who requires a lot of branch service is more expensive to serve (and thus less profitable, all other things equal) than a customer who relies heavily on the online channel for service. But this behavior can change over time — and in both directions. Younger consumers, who may rely heavily on the online channel today, may have more sophisticated needs in the future, and change the channel mix of their interactions over time. And older consumers can be trained and incented to use the online channel, even if they don't today.

The key point is that CLV — which Jim Novo rightly notes is a calculation at a certain point in time — incorporates assumptions about future behavior.[21] The "risk" that this behavior could change should be built into the CLV calculation.

2) Use activity-based costing (ABC). I used channel behavior as an example of a factor impacting customer profitability. But understanding actual channel behavior is a challenge for most firms, as is understanding the true cost of serving customers.

Without ABC, costs are often allocated based on product ownership because service behavior is accepted as an unknown. In some firms — even where service activity is incorporated into CLV estimates — differences in the costs of providing service across channels and even the differences in costs of different types of services is washed over.

Without ABC, marketers can't get an actionable estimate of CLV.

3) Use CLV to drive customer relationship strategies. Somewhere along the line, it became fashionable to say that firms should "fire" unprofitable customers. Unfortunately, firing unprofitable customers is a flawed concept.

As I alluded to in point #2, few marketers can be 100% sure that their CLV calculation is accurate in the first place. But a customer — unprofitable or not — contributes to meeting fixed costs. If you drop unprofitable customers, you (negatively) affect the profitability of other customers — potentially pushing them in front of the "firing squad." And the cycle continues.

In the end, marketers cannot simply use the CLV calculation as the only dimension upon which they segment customers. Even good-old RFM metrics can help better segment customers in order to drive marketing strategies. In the financial services world (where purchase frequency is low), I advocate using customer engagement measures to help provide a qualitative perspective on customer behavior and strategic directions.

Why Firms Don't Care About CLV

On his Marketing Productivity blog, Jim Novo asserts that there are fundamental reasons why companies don't take a longer-term view in respect to their marketing programs including:[22]

- **Business culture** — where performance rewards are tied to short-term goals.

- **Nobody in charge** — no one has full-time responsibility for customer productivity or retention.

- **Lack of desperation** — firms just not feeling the pain (yet).

My take: I agree with Jim 100% — but I think the fundamental reasons go further. The even more fundamental reason is religion. Thesaurus.com defines religion as "a specific fundamental set of beliefs and practices generally agreed upon by a number of persons."

For my money, the reason that LTV hasn't taken hold in many firms is that the marketers in charge have a fundamentally different set of beliefs. This is the essence of marketing's civil war — the branding religion is currently the predominant religion.

The missionaries may very well be right — LTV may be the one right way, and a superior way of (marketing) life. But for now, they're preaching to the choir, and trying to convert the heathen.

Look at the state of "customer engagement." A year ago the ARF defined engagement as "turning on a prospect to a brand idea enhanced by the surrounding context." There are far more articles about how engagement is about how much time someone spends interacting with an ad than how engagement could be about engaging with the product or service itself.

In a recent presentation I made at a marketing conference, as I was discussing customer engagement (a series of interactions that strengthen a customer's emotional connection to a firm), you'd think that many direct marketers had never even heard the term before.

Culture, responsibilities, and economic conditions all definitely play a role. But below that surface are religious differences in marketing theory.

☺ Common Marketing Afflictions

I've detected what appear to be some common afflictions that marketers suffer from. I haven't found the cures yet, I'm still diagnosing the problems. Here's what I've found so far:

Delusions of brandeur. A condition where marketers think that a branding effort will be the antidote to falling or stagnant sales. Showing sufferers pictures of babies, and explaining that their branding effort needs to be nurtured and cared for, has been known to minimize the delusions.

Net promoter syndrome. Sufferers of this "disease" believe that as long as the number of people who will recommend your company is outgrowing the number of people who hate your guts and will stop at nothing to destroy you, then you're on the path to increased profitability and growth. Recent attempts to help sufferers come to grip with the affliction have been ignored.

Calcuphobia. These marketers display an intense dislike — and even fear — of trying to calculate the ROI on their marketing investments. Advanced sufferers don't even bother to track what they've spent in the first place. This is often a sister condition to those who suffer from the first affliction listed above.

Channel vision. Those afflicted with this widespread and debilitating condition believe that the channel they're responsible for is the only channel driving sales and profitability. Not uncommon among those working in eCommerce and mass media advertising.

Blogophilia. Wikipedia defines this as "the irrational belief that creating a blog will, in and of itself, help a company improve its customer relationships." OK, I made that up. But you have to admit, it sounded real — as do so many of the other half-truths floating around Wikipedia.

Extinctivitis. Sadly, marketers suffering from this condition fail to recognize the importance of the online channel to their firm's marketing efforts, let alone the potential impact of Web 2.0 technologies. Oddly, they have a tendency to collect America Online installation CDs from the 90s.

These are a few of the marketing afflictions I've come across. Perhaps you've found some more.

SECTION 7: NET PROMOTER SCORE

Stop Measuring Your Net Promoter Score

Every few years, a new management approach catches on, spreads like wildfire, and produces a small army of disciples, who fall over themselves to christen the new approach the greatest management development since Frederick Taylor did his stopwatch studies.

The early 1990s gave us reengineering, the late 90s produced knowledge management, and in the latter half of the first decade of the new millennium, it's the Net Promoter Score.

A number of observers have eloquently weighed in on the weaknesses of Fred Reichheld's Net Promoter Score. I'll go one step further: Firms should stop measuring their NPS. Why? Because the NPS:

1) Doesn't help explain WHY a customer would recommend the firm. Let's say a bank finds out that 10% of its branches score much higher than the average on the NPS and that 10% score much lower. What has it learned? Nothing. It isn't actionable. You might argue that it provides clues as to where to dig in… but wouldn't it be more useful to find out the root causes in the first place?

2) Measures intention, not behavior. If there's one thing market research has taught us, it's that consumers don't always do what they say they'll do. What's important to firms is who is actually refers the company to their friends and family — not who might do so.

3) Doesn't capture inherent consumer differences. Forrester Research has found that Gen X and Gen Yers are more likely to recommend a firm to their family and friends than Baby Boomers. So if your NPS increases from one year to the next, is it because you improved the products and services you deliver, or does it reflect an underlying change in the demographics of your customer base?

4) Can incent undesirable behavior. One marketing exec told me about an interaction he had at his car dealer's repair shop. When he arrived to pick up his car, the shop manager said "if there's any reason you wouldn't check off the 'likely to recommend' box on the customer satisfaction survey, please let me know before filling out the survey." Do you want your firm's personnel running around asking customers to say they'd refer the firm to friends and family — or doing the things that earn a referral?

5) Uses funds better deployed elsewhere. Measurement doesn't come for free. Firms that have built an infrastructure to measure customer satisfaction are now being encouraged to build an infrastructure around measuring NPS. It's not worth it. There are better things to measure — like what causes a customer to refer a firm in the first place.

It's been said that you can't manage what you don't measure. But a metric that doesn't help you manage isn't worth measuring. And the Net Promoter Score is a measure that doesn't help you manage.

The Great Customer Advocacy Hoax

The Journal of Marketing published a report by Tim Keiningham of IPSOS-Loyalty and others called "A Longitudinal Examination of Net Promoter and Firm Revenue Growth that is gaining currency among NPS bashers.[23] It concludes that:

"We find no support for the claim that Net Promoter is the single most reliable indicator of a company's ability to grow. We found that when making 'apples-to-apples' comparisons, Net Promoter does not perform better than the ACSI. Managers have adopted the Net Promoter metric on the basis that is superior to other metrics. Our research suggests that such presumptions are erroneous."

This study has important implications for firms considering whether or not to adopt the NPS metric as worthy of measurement. For me, though, the issue isn't whether or not NPS is a better metric than customer satisfaction.

The first issue is about money. Measurement costs money.

Over the years, many companies have built an infrastructure around measuring customer satisfaction. Yet, on the urgings of ONE book, a growing number of firms have gone out and spent millions more to measure a new metric. Where's the ROI on that investment? Was this the best place to spend a firm's limited funds? I don't think so, but go ahead — try to convince me that it was.

My second issue is with how the NPS groupies define customer advocacy — as the customer "advocating" for the company through a willingness to provide referrals to family and friends. Few people seem willing to see customer advocacy through another lens: The perception on the part of the customer that a firm does what's best for the customer, and not just its own bottom line.

This is how Forrester Research defines it, which publishes an annual Customer Advocacy ranking of financial firms. Overshadowed by the rankings is a key finding: Across the banking, brokerage, and insurance arenas, consumers that rate their financial providers as doing what's best for the customer are far more likely to consider buying from those firms in the future.

The third issue is the lack of theories about causality. Neither the NPS nor ACSI supporters make a case for why their favorite metric drives growth.

Which is why I like Forrester's definition of advocacy. It implies that if you do what's right for your customer — or at least create that impression — then it will result in satisfied customers who refer the firm to friends and family. And create customers who want to do more business in the future.

Maybe someday more execs will come around to this way of thinking. In the meantime, I guess we'll just have to live the NPS groupies' great customer advocacy hoax.

The ONE Question To Ask Customers

Many firms (financial services firms, in particular) segment their customer base using a "value" approach, segmenting customers by their value to the firm — looking at the number of products owned, or estimating profitability. Others use psychographic approaches to identify the differences among customers as they relate to attitudes about life in general or about managing their financial lives.

But both of these approaches, however, fail to identify the type of relationship a customer wants to have with the firm.

Consumers enter into "relationships" with firms with different expectations — and desires — for what that relationship will be. I put the word in quotes, because in some (many?) cases, a consumer doesn't want a relationship — he simply wants to buy and use a product or service from the firm. But as marketers, we're looking to deepen the relationship our customers have with us.

So, what's the one question to ask customers?

What are your expectations of us and how well are we meeting those expectations?

The challenge is in constructing the right prompts for the expectations question. From research I've done with financial services consumers, I strongly believe that many consumers' expectations will fall into one of the following buckets:

- **Interpersonal excellence.** These are the consumers who are predominantly looking to deal with employees who are friendly and helpful; take the time to listen to problems, concerns, and needs; and live up to values portrayed in the firm's ads.

- **Advice and guidance.** These consumers are expecting objective advice and guidance in making product decisions and making the best use of those products. They may or may not care if the people they deal with are "friendly", and they may not care if the advice and guidance they get even comes from a human (versus a Web site).

- **Operational excellence.** These consumers want to do business with a firm that's easy to do business with and never makes mistakes. Again, they may or not care if the people they deal with are "friendly and helpful" — in fact, they probably don't even want to talk to those people in the first place.

If you don't know what your customers expect from you — and how well you meet those expectations, then: 1) you can't know what you have to do to grow the relationship, and 2) who cares if they'll refer you to their friends and family?

Announcing A New NPS Metric

Sufferers from Net Promoter Syndrome share a symptom with those afflicted with a marketing malady called Simplificosis, the tendency to believe that just because a metric is simpler to understand or measure than other metrics, then it must be better.

I understand that companies often make things more difficult than they need to be and that simplification has its benefits.

Example: Applying for a mortgage. The complex way: Fill out a 15 page form and wait 3 weeks for an answer. The simple way: Answer 3 questions (name, address of the home you're buying, and how much money do you make) and get your answer immediately.

But sometimes, simplification isn't an improvement.

Example: Getting directions from Boston to New York. The complex way: Take the Mass Pike to the Rte 84 exit, merge onto Rte 15 south towards I-91, go east on .... and so on. The simple way: Go southwest.

Correct, simpler, but not exactly an improvement.

This is the trap that Net Promoter Syndrome sufferers fall into. Paul Marsden wrote "the simplicity of the model…has made research intelligible at the board level."

It's intelligible, however, not because it's right, but because Reichheld knows how to communicate with senior management. I hate to say it, but many market researchers don't. Citing margins of error, R-squared scores, etc. doesn't resonate with a lot of execs.

But the reality of NPS is that it's not that simple. Common practice is to consider customers as promoters if they give a 9 or 10 on the 10-point scale. But in comparing NPS between time periods, it's possible that the net score could increase while a significant number of customers shift from 7s and 8s to 1s and 2s. Not so simple.

Bottom line: Simpler doesn't mean better, nor does it make it "more right" than complex.

But if it's simpler you want, it's simpler you'll get. Here's a new metric for you. And since it might be too complex for some people to remember a new acronym, my new metric will keep the NPS moniker. Announcing the new NPS:

Net Purchaser Score: The net difference between the number of people who bought your product and the number of people who returned it.

I just know that my NPS will correlate with revenue and profitability growth. And the beauty of my metric is that it:

1. Measures behavior (not intention)
2. Encompasses all customers (not just a sample)
3. Directly impacts the bottom line (not indirectly)
4. Can be measured in real-time (or at least more often than surveys)
5. Is simple!

As soon as I finish the research, I'll expect all the Net Promoter promoters to drop their support of their metric, since something better — and simpler — will have come along.

What Does The Marketing Science Institute's Award Say About Net Promoter Score?

Tim Keiningham and his colleagues won the 2007 Marketing Science Institute/H. Paul Root Award given to the Journal of Marketing paper that had "the most significant contribution to the advancement of the practice of marketing." To quote from the paper:

"We find no support for the claim that Net Promoter is the single most reliable indicator of a company's ability to grow. We found that when making 'apples-to-apples' comparisons, Net Promoter does not perform better than the ACSI. Managers have adopted the Net Promoter metric on the basis that is superior to other metrics. Our research suggests that such presumptions are erroneous."

My take: If the Marketing Science Institute says that the "most significant contribution to the advancement of the practice of marketing" is a study that refutes one of today's most popular marketing fads, namely the Net Promoter Score, what does this say for the credibility and long-term success of NPS?

It says that the beginning of the end has begun. Management fads go through a predictable cycle of four stages. They:

- Begin to show up in the management press with articles (or books) from early proponents;

- Gain acceptance when credible case studies highlight the [allegedly] superior performance firms realize from deploying the concept;

- Come under more rigorous scrutiny which produces studies and examples that refute and challenge the claims of success; and then

- Begin a decline in popularity (but can become part of the fabric of management if — and only if — they're truly a worthwhile concept).

In addition to the Keiningham study, comes stories like this from blogger Paul Schwartz:[24]

"I've been using NPS with clients for a couple of years, and I'm not convinced yet that it is the best indicator of a company's ability to grow. The real work is figuring out what drives the likelihood to recommend for each business, and then measuring the actual recommendation and purchase behavior of customers."

Not convinced yet, Paul? You may never be. More studies like Keiningham's will be done, and more stories like yours will be told in 2008. 2008 will be the year that NPS moves into stage 3.

Word-Of-Mouth Recommendations

Research about word-of-mouth recommendations from Nanyang Technological University and the University of British Columbia should be of interest to financial services marketers.[25] According to the study:

"Consumers are more likely to provide WOM for products that are relevant to self-concept than for more utilitarian products. There was some indication that…consumers exaggerated the benefits of self-relevant products compared to utilitarian products."

Why is this important to banks? Because financial service products don't fit neatly into either the "self-concept" or "utilitarian" categories.

Some consumers are highly involved in managing their financial lives and making financial decisions, and are more likely to consider financial services products (like checking accounts, brokerage accounts, mutual funds owned) as relevant to their self-concept. For other consumers, these products may be utilitarian ("my checking account is nothing more than a place to stick my money before paying it out to everybody I have to pay").

Smart banks know that customer referrals are an important source of new business. This research should lead them to address a few questions:

- **Can we convert customers from "utilitarian" to "self-concept"?** A bank that successfully does this may not only drive up referrals, but increase the level of engagement that the customer has with the bank, leading to increased purchases from that customer.

- **What does our customer base look like?** Do the majority of our customers take a utilitarian view versus a self-concept one? Why? Are we better at attracting one type of customer than another?

- **What should we measure?** As banks (as well as many other firms) adopt the Net Promoter Score methodology, this WOM research begs the question: Is the NPS more a reflection of the underlying demographics of the customer base than the performance of the bank?

My bet is that some other metric — like customer engagement or customer lifetime value — does a better job of capturing the self-concept/utilitarian dichotomy and is a better metric to guide decision making.

Word-Of-Mouth Could Use A Shot Of Collagen

A Forrester Research survey of 5,000 US households found that 46% of consumers don't give advice about products to their friends and family.[26]

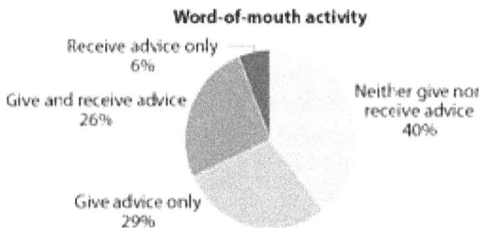

Word-of-mouth activity

Receive advice only
6%

Give and receive advice
26%

Neither give nor
receive advice
40%

Give advice only
29%

Base: 5,005 US households
(numbers may not total 100 due to rounding)
Source: Forrester's North American Consumer Technology Adoption Study 2006 Benchmark Survey

Let's put this statistic in some perspective. According to Net Promoter (the "Official Net Promoter Web Site"), Saturn, for example, has a Net Promoter score of 74%. This means that, at a minimum, 74% of its customers are Promoters (if not a single customer was a Detractor).

But if nearly half of all consumers don't give product advice, then how could Saturn (not to mention other firms) have that many consumers who are highly likely to recommend those firms to their friends and colleagues?

I've come up with three possible explanations:

1) **Saturn's customers are different.** From a demographic, psychographic, attitudinal, behavioral, etc. perspective, Saturn's customers might look more like the 54% who do give product advice. Unfortunately, that explanation holds no water. According to

Forrester, the demographics of WOM customers (those who do provide advice) are nearly identical to those who don't provide advice.

2) **Forrester's respondents are lying.** It's possible. But it's highly unlikely that that many respondents would lie about something like this. The real number may a couple of percentage points lower — but could be higher, as well.

3) **People apply their own interpretation to the question.** I'm a Forrester client, and an avid reader of the research. Online versions of the research ask "how likely is it that you would recommend this document to a colleague"? I've never recommended a document to a colleague. But I have rated plenty of documents a 10. Why? Because it's the only way for me to express my opinion. Forrester doesn't ask me if I like the document, or if I'm happy or satisfied with it — which is what I'd rather be telling them about.

And so when Net Promoter Syndrome sufferers ask their one question — would you recommend us? — it's possible that respondents are rating the firm a 9 or 10, not because they would recommend the firm, but simply because they're looking to express their — gasp — satisfaction with the firm.

And not only is this possible, but my bet is that it's likely.

☺ Identifying The Psychopathicos In Your Customer Base

First, we had Net Promoter Syndrome sufferers telling marketers that they had to figure out which of their customers were "advocates", that is, those who gave a top-two box rating on a 10-point scale of likelihood to recommend the firm to friends, families, household pets, trees, and other living creatures.

Now, Yahoo! is telling us we have to identify the "passionistas" are among our customer base.[27] According to Yahoo!, passionistas are "natural advocates and already online creating and sharing content about their passions and brands that align with them."

So what's next? I have the answer. Marketers must identify the Psychopathicos among their customer base.

Psychopathicos: Customers who will hurt, maim, or kill anybody who refuses to buy your products and services. They don't just refer your firm to their friends and neighbors — they force them to buy from you.

"You don't like Coke, you Pepsi pansy? You will after I whack you upside the head with this 64-oz. bottle of Coke!"

You think your Net Promoter Score is correlated to growth? Ha! Your market share will *skyrocket* with every 1% improvement in your firm's Psychopathico Index (which, by the way, I can help you measure for a measly six-figure consulting fee).

I just don't want to be there for the focus group study.

SECTION 8: CUSTOMER LOYALTY

The Stories Loyal Customers Tell

From the market research studies I've been involved with, I've heard the following stories from loyal financial services customers:

#1: A man in his late-50s, when asked by his bank in a focus group interview why he was a loyal customer, hemmed and hawed for a few moments before saying "it's because of Jenny, the branch manager where I bank." When asked what made Jenny so special, he replied, "I don't know. But one time I came into the branch to make a deposit, and the pen at the counter was out of ink. Although Jenny had a customer in with her, she somehow knew that pen was out of ink, and came out with a batch of new pens. That's Jenny for you."

#2: A magazine reporter and her partner were trying to adopt a child, and had received word from the adoption agency that a child was available for adoption. But they needed a short term loan in order to make the trip to China to pick up the baby. According to the reporter, her bank "bent over backwards to approve the loan and get her the money in 24 hours" and for that she would "never leave them."

#3: An IT executive traces his loyalty to USAA back to a single phone call. He called the firm to cancel a credit card and insurance policy. The rep said "I hope I'm not overstepping my boundaries, but we've found that many customers often cancel products because of events that aren't related to USAA like a divorce or other family matter. We've set up a special department to help customers with these kinds of matters, is this something we might be able to help you with?" Since he was in the middle of the divorce, he took USAA up on that offer and has been a loyal customer since.

These may sound like unrelated stories, but there are lessons to be gleaned:

- **It takes more than just "great customer service".** Consumers have different expectations of the firms they do business with, one of them being "interpersonal excellence." The man in story #1 is an example of this. It wasn't any single interaction that drove his loyalty to the bank — it was the personal attention he received from Jenny and the connection he had with her.

- **Convenience isn't enough.** For banking customers, the added convenience of late branch hours or multiple ATM locations may be important, but the produce the stories that customers tell. In story #2, it was the bank's operational excellence — its ability to turn the loan app around in 24 hours — than helped produce the story that woman tells.

- **It's the high-emotion interactions that count the most.** Examples #2 and #3 highlight the fact that stories are more likely to be formed during highly emotional situations — like a loan application or divorce. [Colin: This is why the JetBlue response to its Valentine's Day travel disaster is so much more important than WordPress' handling of down time. Sitting around an airport is much more stressful than waiting for your blog site to come up]. McKinsey calls these "moments-of-truth". The challenge many banks — and other firms — have is recognizing these high-emotion interactions when they happen.

So what should Marketing do?

1) Strategerize its "test and learn" agenda. That's what USAA did. It posed the question: Why do customers leave? (NOT: What can we do to try and salvage a defection — when it's too late to do so)? Analytics execs should reexamine their group's test and learn agenda to determine if they're really asking the important strategic questions — or just refining their knowledge of campaign-level results. (This is a good example of Marketing focusing more on the "macro" and less on the "micro").

2) **Better integrate.** The advertising folks use the term "integrated marketing" to refer to ad campaigns that are coordinated (or the same) across channels. That's all well and fine, but for many marketing departments the bigger challenge is internal integration — and one prime example is the need for integration between analytics and market research. The two groups need to work a whole lot closer to develop and test theories about customer behavior.

3) **Redefine customer segments.** The stories that customers tell are clues into their expectations and the drivers of their satisfaction. Firms that continue to define customer segments by products owned or profitability miss these clues — clues that are more valuable to understanding how to sell and service customers than product propensity models that predict what to sell.

Wall Street Discovers Customer Loyalty

A recent segment on CNBC posed the question: Is there something investors should consider beyond the numbers? The suggested answer: Customer loyalty. As if it were a new concept.

The discussion with three customer loyalty "experts" (in quotes because one guy was from a firm that help telcos/IT firms develop qualified new sales and new market opportunities", and the other two were from Wall Street investment houses) contained a few questionable comments and perpetuates some common misconceptions about customer loyalty. According to the experts:

"Most companies spend millions of dollars on sales and marketing but very little money on retaining the customers they just sold to."

My take: Ah, the old myth about the cost of acquisition versus the cost of retention. Apparently, the costs that firms incur to provide customer service to existing customers don't count as retaining them. And direct marketing efforts to cross-sell customers don't count. And from a B2B perspective, the costs associated with providing account management must not qualify. The notion that firms spend little on retention is flat-out wrong.

"While customer loyalty is important, it's no substitute for strong operational performance."

My take: First off, this misses the point that for some firms/brands, it's strong operational performance that earned the loyalty in the first place. But second, if a brand has strong loyalty, shouldn't that compensate for less than stellar operational performance? I think what the expert was trying to say was that loyalty wasn't a substitute for strong financial performance. In other words, it doesn't matter if you have raving fans — just make your quarterly numbers.

"In tough times, price matters. To maintain a brand, firms have to spend an enormous amount of money."

My take: If a customer's loyalty is that susceptible to economic conditions, it's got to make you wonder how strong the loyalty is. For example, if a "loyal" Starbucks customer switches from Starbucks to Dunkin' Donuts for her daily caffeine fix during a downturn, then how loyal was she to Starbucks in the first place? If, on the other hand, she only buys coffee every other day — but still buys it from Starbucks — then the loyalty is still strong, even though total sales volume is down.

The problem with Wall Street's view of customer loyalty is that it confuses:

1) Customer loyalty with brand affinity. When asked which firms have strong customer loyalty, all of the experts agreed on Apple. No doubt that many Apple customers are vocal supporters of the firm. But there are a lot of firms out whose customers don't buy from anybody else. Strong brand affinity may breed loyal behavior, but you can still have loyalty without the strong brand affinity.

2) Retention with share of wallet. Firms that sell products or services with low purchase frequency often fall prey to this misconception. Just because a bank customer isn't motivated enough to go searching for a new checking account provider, it doesn't mean he's loyal to his bank. Likewise, if he stays with his bank for his checking account, but parks all his investments with other firms, then how loyal is he to the bank? Not very.

3) Ad spend with marketing spend. This isn't just a Wall Street issue, it's a Madison Avenue issue, as well. There are way too many people who seem to forget that advertising is under the marketing umbrella — and not the other way around. There are a lot of marketing investments that firms make beyond advertising. But go tell that to the advertising people.

4) The means with the ends. Apple isn't great because it has raving fans. It's great because it's great at product design, which attracts customers who appreciate and value product design. This is, perhaps, a not-so-subtle point, but one that many firms miss. Instead of saying "let's go improve our customer loyalty" firms should be saying "let's be great at something that customers will value and therefore be loyal to us."

I'm really looking forward to Wall Street's next great insight.

Looking For Love (Loyalty) In All The Wrong Places (Customers)

Economist Umair Hague makes an interesting point — and raises some interesting questions — about customer and brand loyalty:[28]

"Why do Apple customers care so much (about Apple)? It's a good question. But in fact, it's the wrong question to start thinking strategically about consumption. The real question is the opposite: Why don't most consumers care more about firms, products, services, and brands?"

My take: One reason why consumers don't care more about the firms/brands is that they don't care that much about the product/service that they purchased from that firm.

This is one of the big hurdles facing financial services marketers looking to engender loyalty among their firms' customer base.

While money is really really important to whole lot of consumers, managing money is not something that a whole lot of consumers like doing or look forward to doing. More importantly (from a loyalty building perspective), it's not something by which they define themselves.

Apple fanatics wear their loyalty like a badge. But how many people consider themselves a "Fifth Third fellow" or a "Chase chap"? (Stop laughing).

Customers have to care enough about the product before they'll care enough about the firm or brand. Few — if any — banks get this.

This is why a community like Wesabe is so important. It's a community of consumers who are involved enough with the management of their financial lives to participate in a community with other like-minded consumers. They're potentially consumers who — despite the conventional wisdom that they're rate hoppers–

might become loyal to a particular financial firm because they're involved enough with the products and services to understand how that firm is different in its product and service delivery capabilities.

Banks have really missed the boat in developing Wesabe-like sites. On one hand, they can't envision where the payback on the investment will come from. They know they can't charge customers for the privilege (stop laughing) to participate. And on the other hand, they're fearful that their customers, left unchecked, might — gasp! — recommend other banks and services to fellow community members.

What they've failed to grasp is that financial community members like Wesabeans (I wonder if anybody actually refers to him or herself as a Wesabean) are hand-raisers. They're people who are demonstrating an interest in their financial lives — and therefore signaling their potential to be a more loyal customer because of their engagement with the product category.

Understanding customers' product category engagement could have huge impact on how a firm executes its marketing programs (in terms of targeted offers and calls to action), segments its customer base, and calculates potential lifetime value (if it calculates it at all).

It's possible to predict category engagement using behavioral data that the bank collects. For example: How many times does an online banking customer check savings rates each quarter? How often has a customer moved money between accounts each quarter? (Interestingly, a customer that frequently moves money out of the institution might be a better candidate for long-term loyalty than a customer who just parks him money there).

Until marketers incorporate category engagement into their marketing efforts, they'll be looking for love…in all the wrong places.

Moments Of Truth

A former colleague of mine had her wallet stolen recently, and she recounted her experience on her blog. Her prescriptions to the firms she had to deal with -- to have empathy and map out process from the customer's perspective -- are right on. Here's what I'd add: They have to identify the moments of truth.

Customer loyalty is driven by the stories customers tell themselves (and not just the "authentic" stories marketers tell customers, Mr. Godin). These stories are born out of the high-emotion interactions that customers have with firms — what McKinsey refers to as "moments of truth."

What the firms my friend dealt didn't recognize was that reporting a lost or stolen card is a highly emotional situation. One that warrants special treatment.

If any of them had immediately put her through to a human who said "I will personally take care of this and help you", she would have glowed about the service. She'd believe that that firm was truly different. Most importantly, it would become a "story a loyal customer tells".

But none of the firms did this. They didn't recognize a moment of truth.

Identifying these moments isn't rocket science. Market research can help you determine which interactions have a higher emotional impact than others. Simple common sense can help, too. Which is probably why my friend said that becoming customer-centric isn't THAT hard.

Trust Is A Two-Way Street

If he wasn't the first to coin the term trust-based marketing, then Glen Urban of MIT was certainly one of the first to write about it and help marketers understand the importance of trust in a customer relationship.[29]

Today, financial firms are embracing this concept — it seems like just about every FI exhorts consumers to "trust us." Unfortunately, their actions don't always live up to their words.

And unfortunately, many firms fail to recognize that trust is a two-way street.

The following is a recent post from a fellow blogger:

"Earlier this month, I spoke with a bank rep about a $592 fraudulent charge that had been posted to my checking acct. I filed a dispute against the merchant and was told it would take approx. 5 business days for the matter to be resolved. In the meantime, I was concerned I would incur insufficient fund fees.

The rep informed me I would be able to file a "separate" dispute once this dispute cleared. Essentially, rack up fees, then we'll credit your acct? Pretty wacked.

Two days later, there was a credit to my acct. for $592. Yeah - problem resolved - or so I thought. I incurred over $300 in insufficient funds fees - Yikes!

As instructed by the rep, I called to file an additional dispute to recover the insufficient funds fees. The rep I filed the original claim with failed to record it on my acct. So they claimed to have no record of a dispute. On top of that, I was informed the (evil) merchant "credited" my acct. for the unauthorized charge.

Since the merchant "credited" my acct, it was no longer considered a fraudulent charge & there was no need for a dispute. What the @%&$?

I got passed off to a manager who informed me the bank wasn't responsible for the insufficient funds fees because there wasn't a record of a dispute. So now you're telling me it's my fault that your people are incompetent?!"

My take: Clearly, a number of things went wrong here. But what strikes me as the most egregious sin, however, is the lack of trust – of the bank in its customer.

Granted, there's a lot of fraudulent activity going on out there. But this bank basically didn't believe its customer when she said she had called to file the claim. In effect, it called her liar.

So here we have a bank, who, if it's like many of the others out there, is telling customers and prospects in its ads and marketing messages to "trust us." And what does it do? Turns around and mistrusts its own customers.

A simple review of this woman's account would likely have provided clues as to whether or not she was trying to commit some fraud. But it should never have even come to that.

The bank — without batting an eyelash — should have apologized and told her it was sorry and that it would credit her account for the fees. And then look into the legitimacy of the situation. We're talking $300 here.

What's sad about this situation is that if this customer is a professional or small business owner, she'll be likely to get cross-sell offers from the bank to open investment accounts or a small business account. And what do you think are the chances that she'll respond to these offers? I wouldn't bet on it.

There are two things about this story that make me shake my head. Apparently, there are still a lot of banks that just don't get that:

1. They have to identify and act on the moments of truth that occur, and

2. To get trust, you have to give trust.

This was a moment of truth. The bank didn't identify it, and (in this case) couldn't rectify it. The result: Maybe not a lost customer, but probably a customer who's unlikely to grow her relationship. And definitely a loss of trust.

Frequent Customer Contact Is A Blessing, Not A Curse

As part of a special section on "Building A Better Customer Experience," American Banker reported the extent to which consumers viewed financial firms as acting in the customer's best interest (in contrast to acting in the interests of its own bottom line). A quote from the managing director of a New York-based consulting firm, explaining why banks scored lower than other types of FIs, caught my eye:

"Most people interact with their banks more often than they do with an insurer or a brokerage, so there is more opportunity for error. People have more frequent contact and more types of contact with their bank, so things like hours and fees seem onerous."

My take: Frequent contact with customers is a blessing, not a curse.

A few years ago, I was speaking at a conference about the impact of online banking on customer loyalty, and I presented the results of a study that Bank of America did that showed that — all else being equal (e.g, demographics, tenure with the bank, starting balances) — over time, online bill pay customers grew balances and number of products owned faster than other customers.

I wondered out loud why that would be — after all, what was it about paying bills online that made someone more loyal to his or her bank?

I found that there are (at least) two possible answers. The first has to do with consumers' motivations and expectations. For some consumers, the strength of the relationship they have with their bank is predominantly driven by factors relating to convenience. As a result, the convenience that they experience by paying bills online strengthens their emotional connection to their bank.

But the second explanation — the one most relevant here— came from someone sitting in on my presentation that day. Neal Burns, a University of Texas at Austin professor of advertising, told me that according to research he's done, "repeated, positive interactions with a brand strengthen a customer's connection to that brand."

Insurers get few chances to create that positive impression — but when they do, they're usually good opportunities, since insurance claims are typically high emotion interactions. Brokerages — particularly discount brokerages — may get that chance even less frequently, especially if they don't have an advisory relationship with the customer.

Banks should be thankful for the frequency of contact they have with their customers. That their scores in the survey are lower than other FIs isn't because of "opportunity for error". It's better attributed to:

- **Organizational conflict.** The product-centric nature of most banks creates conflicting goals and incentives that make it difficult for those firms to always act in a customer's best interest. Can we really expect a mortgage specialist to tell a checking account customer that he might get a better deal on a loan by going across the street?

- **A focus on the wrong experiences.** I don't mean to downplay the importance of customer service interactions, but I believe that the scores reported in American Banker reflect the dissatisfaction and missed expectations that consumers have with their sales experiences. It's in these interactions where they receive product recommendations that they perceive to be best for the bank and not for them, and where their expectations of what it's like to do business with the bank are established. Expectations that, in some cases, are not lived up to.

Banks that build trust with their customers earn forgiveness when (and if) they do make a mistake. Having the opportunity to build that trust through frequent interactions is a firm's advantage — not handicap.

Which Is Better: Emotional Or Informational Advertising?

Researchers from three Washington universities found that:[30]

"Consumers who are skeptical about the truth of advertising claims are more responsive to emotionally appealing ads than ones peppered with information."

Emotional ads were characterized as "providing an emotional experience that is relevant to the use of the brand; informational ads predominantly provide clear brand data."

Although these findings might not apply to all products, the research does have important implications for financial services marketers.

Today's financial services consumers are skeptical. But in financial firms' zeal to make an emotional connection with consumers through their ads, many have failed to meet one of the stipulations of the research study: Relevance.

Financial services firms seem to be falling over each these days, promising to help consumers "achieve [reach, fulfill] their dreams." But this emotional plea falls short of being an "experience relevant to the use of the brand."

Rather than asking "what emotional connection can we make through our advertising?", financial firms need to understand "what emotional connection are we good at making today?"

They would find that emotional connections vary by customer. Some make an emotional connection based on the interpersonal relationships they have with the firm, some become attached because of the objective guidance and advice they receive, while others are driven by the convenience and operational effectiveness they experience.

Few consumers (and I'm being generous), when asked about their bank or brokerage, would say "they helped me achieve my dreams."

Back to the ad storyboard, financial services firms.

☺ Advertising On Airport Security Bins

Advertising on airport security bins is a brilliant idea. Here's who should advertise there (and their message):

Handi Wipes. "Cuz' God knows what's been put in these bins."

Banks. "Bank with us. Our lines are shorter than this one."

Amtrak. "If you rode the train you wouldn't need this bin [well, not yet]."

Cialis. "By the time you get through this line, Viagra will have worn off. With Cialis, you'll still have 34 hours to go."

Geico. "Got 15 minutes? Hell, you've got 115 minutes!"

DeBeers. "Diamonds are forever. Which is about how long it took you to get through this line."

Microsoft. "Where do you want to go today? (Not that it matters — you're not going anywhere!)"

American Express. "Don't leave home without it."

Capital One. "What's in your wallet? (Never mind, we're about to find out)."

Travelex. "Did you see what the guy in front of you put in here? Travelex travel insurance kiosks — Gate 17."

SECTION 9: WEB 2.0

The Unrealized ROI Of Blogging

Forrester Research published a report on the ROI of blogging featuring a case study on the ROI of General Motors' FastLane blog.[31]

According to Forrester, GM's first-year ROI on the blog was 99%. The primary contributors to the top line: 1) $180,000 in customer insight, which was estimated by assuming a cost of $15,000 for running a monthly focus group with 10 participants over the course of a year, and 2) $380,000 in press coverage, calculated by estimating the value of "high-visibility Web placements" and the cost of CPM advertising on sites like InformationWeek.

My take: Few firms will get *anywhere* close to those returns. Why? Few, if any, will stop running focus groups or advertisements. ROI estimates based on cost displacement are only realized if the expenses to be displaced don't get spent. Two implications for marketing execs:

1) Budgeting and investment allocation decisions that exist within departmental silos are practically guaranteed to prevent cost displacements that occur outside that department (talk to your IT folks, they know all about this), and

2) If you're going to tout the potential ROI of blogging to your CEO, you'd better be ready to make some tough decisions about where the money to fund the effort is going to come from (talk to your analytics folks, they should be able to help you here).

Should You Blog? What Jakob Nielsen Got Wrong

Well-known usability expert Jakob Nielsen, writing in his weekly Alertbox, said:[32]

"I recently served as a "consultant's consultant," advising a world leader in his field on what to do about his website. In particular, this expert asked me whether he should start a weblog. I said no. I recommended that he should instead invest his time in writing thorough articles that he published on a regular schedule. Given limited time, this means not spending the effort to post numerous short comments on ongoing blogosphere discussions."

Did Mr. Nielsen give the right advice?

Judging by the comments on blogs like Scobleizer and Marketing Roadmaps, there may quite a few people who don't think so. Personally, I don't think he was right — but I don't think he was wrong. I think he had NO RIGHT GIVING THE ADVICE in the first place.

If I were asked by a "world leader" — or a "world loser", for that matter — whether or not s/he should start a blog, I wouldn't give an answer. I would ask a question: What are you trying to accomplish?

Imagine for a moment that I'm a world leader on some topic (stop laughing and try harder). That implies that I've already established some credibility in my field, that quite possibly came about by publishing "thorough articles" on a regular basis.

But what if I said I was dissatisfied with the exposure my white papers or articles have, or that I was dissatisfied with the extent to which I was connected to my audience on a day to day basis? With this assumption, creating a blog might be appropriate advice.

If, on the other hand, I was intimately involved on a regular basis with my clients and prospects, but was perceived as too tactical and not strategic enough, then not creating a blog might be an appropriate response. Maybe.

My point is this: You can't determine whether or not a blog is appropriate for your firm without first clearly defining the objectives you're trying to achieve.

And any consultant that provides a recommendation without first asking about those objectives is irresponsible and possibly incompetent.

What Makes A Blog Credible?

Part 1: The Data

I was searching for a research study I had seen years ago, when I stumbled upon one conducted by BJ Fogg and his colleagues at Stanford's Persuasion Technology Lab (love that name) about the factors that determine consumers' perceptions of what makes a Web site credible.

The study found that there are five composite scales that contribute to credibility, and two that detract from it. Credibility builders include:

- **Real-world feel.** This includes providing quick responses to customer service questions, providing contact phone numbers and email addresses, and showing photos of the firm's employees.

- **Ease-of-use.** Positive impacts on this scale include the ability to search through past content and a professional design. Difficult navigation is a major detractor to ease-of-use.

- **Expertise.** Sites that list credentials demonstrate expertise according to the study. Interestingly, displaying awards was not a strong determinant of expertise.

- **Trustworthiness.** People trust sites that are linked by other sites they find trustworthy. Linking to other sources and materials — including competitors — also builds trustworthiness.

- **Tailoring.** The strongest factor contributing to this scale was sending emails confirming transactions made. Surprisingly, recognizing past visitors was not a strong contributor to an overall tailoring score.

The two scales that diminish site credibility are:

- **Commercial implications.** Sites that make it hard to distinguish ads from content score high (not good) on this scale. Popping up new windows with ads also contribute strongly to this negative rating.

- **Amateurism.** Rarely updating the site with new content, linking to non-credible sites, broken links, and typos all contribute strongly to this negative factor.

My take: These same Web site credibility-building (and detracting) factors also apply to blogs.

Clearly, there are some strong parallels. Instead of quick responses to customer service questions, credible bloggers provide quick responses to visitor comments. The impact of a professional design should be taken seriously by those of us who rely on Blogger or Wordpress for blog design. And I found the "commercial implications" factor particularly interesting, because of a pet peeve I have with blogs cluttered with so many Google ads that I have trouble finding, let alone reading, the content.

Part 2: The Confession

I have a confession to make. The research study I originally was looking for talked about how pictures of employees on Web sites builds trust with site visitors. I went looking for it because there's a credit union blog I visit regularly that shows pictures of the site contributors — as children. And I have to admit that the pictures bug me to no end (I want to see what they look like today — not 20 or 30 years ago).

I wanted to find the data to prove to the credit union that while employee pictures were good — employee pictures as children were bad. Alas, I didn't find that study, so I have no empirical data to support my opinion.

Part 3: The Revelation

It's just as well that I couldn't find the study I was looking for. Because two things dawned on me. First off, it doesn't matter what I think — I'm not a member of the credit union, nor am I likely to become one. So if the pictures bug me, it's my tough luck.

More importantly, though, was my second revelation: The kiddie pictures support the CU's members' cross-channel experience. Members that visit the site and see the kiddie pictures probably comment on them when they meet those CU associates in the branches. The pictures are a conversation starter — a mechanism for engaging members.

I don't know if the folks at the credit union consciously thought about that when they decided to put their kiddie pictures on the blog (they're probably reading this saying "of course we did!"). But for financial firms (credit unions or banks) looking to develop relationships with its customers, anything that gives them an opportunity to put a personal touch on their interactions with customers — and increase engagement — is a good thing.

After all, there's got to be a good reason why Facebook is more popular than Textbook.

Blogs And Banks

Jupiter Research published a report called "Blogs and Banks: Prioritizing Blog-Based Marketing Initiatives to Gain Maximum Effect."[33] In addition to advising banks to advertise on third-party blogs, it recommends that banks:

- Create a blog as part of a young consumer-focused marketing initiative.

- Explore the creation of community-focused blogs.

- Use blogs to promote products — but to "use care."

My take: In addition to my objections regarding the imprecise advice (what does it mean to "explore" the creation of blogs or to "use care" when creating product-focused blogs?), I've got issues with the recommendations concerning:

1) Advertising. Most banks struggle to determine the ROI of their marketing spend. In an environment where direct mail expenditures are scrutinized for their net (not just gross) return, diverting funds to blogvertise is foolish.

Will large banks drive more traffic to their sites by advertising on third-party blogs? I don't think so. Will they gain street cred by blogvertising? Doubtful.

And which blogs was Jupiter referring to? My site is a third-party blog — should a bank like Wells Fargo advertise here? I think not. [Note to Wells Fargo: I'd be more than happy to take your money should you disagree and want to advertise on my site].

2) Strategy. Deploying a blog "in support of a marketing initiative" really misses the boat on the blogging opportunity.

Jupiter cited a student contest run by Royal Bank of Canada which generated "over 20 comments" (translation: 21) during the six months the blog was active. While the bank might call this a successful campaign, it falls short of the potential to utilize blogs, and is a poor example — not a best practice — for other banks to follow.

Creating strong relationships — whether in our personal lives or between companies and customers — requires interaction and dialogue. This is the power of blogs that didn't exist in the world of mass marketing — the opportunity to engage customers in a personal dialogue. Subordinating a blog to a marketing initiative (campaign) is exactly what banks should avoid doing.

There's nothing wrong with focusing blogging efforts on today's young consumers. But banks have an opportunity to do something with this group that they haven't been able to do with older generations — build a mutually trusting relationship. It would be a shame to use Boomer- and Senior-like marketing tactics to engage banks' future customer base.

Seven or eight years ago, when the first wave of online communities popped up, a number of banks tried their hand at creating forums to engage their customers in community-related topics. For the most part, those efforts failed miserably.

You might argue that they were ahead of their time. I'd argue that few consumers wanted to engage in community-related discussions with their big, impersonal bank who was likely to be acquired by some even-bigger bank. And that hasn't changed.

The bigger question is can a bank build trust by establishing a community-focused blog, or must it build trust first, before it can be successful with a community-focused blog? My money is on the latter.

The Question Isn't Should Banks Blog, But How And When

Javelin Research said:[34]

"Banks should move fast to open their blog sites if they are not to miss out on a powerful new brand building and customer interaction capability."

My take: Whoa, not so fast.

You don't have to convince me of the potential for banks (or other types of firms) to use blogs to engage customers, strengthen the relationship, and build true customer loyalty.

But you can't simply put up a site and say "here we are! we have a blog!"

For many firms, simply doing that is likely to produce one of the following:

1. Deafening silence as nobody participates.

2. Deafening noise as customers rant about their service issues.

Or possibly something in between (but closer to the first) as a few employees (maybe even the CEO) post a few entries, and a few comments trickle in.

The challenges that many banks face in trying to build strong customer relationships aren't going to be overcome simply by blogging. A blog has a better chance of helping when you already have a set of engaged customers, or at least, customers inclined to engage with the bank.

On top of that is the question of blog strategy and execution. There are two good examples to use to contrast different approaches: Wells Fargo and Verity Credit Union. Wells has created four distinct blogs, each with a distinct topic focus. Verity, in contrast, has a single blog, covering a range of topics determined by the contributor.

Both are excellent sites, but accomplish very different objectives. The common thread is a set of contributors, who, although maybe not dedicated to the blogging effort, are certainly highly committed to it.

So let me ask you this, budding blogger….are there employees in your firm chomping at the bit to blog, and who will invest time on top of their existing workload?

On what topics do you expect to blog about? Everything under the sun or just certain things? And why would your customers care what you have to say about those topics?

And which customers, exactly, will come flocking to your blog to converse, fall in love with you, and give you all their money? Baby boomers, who trust you about as far as they can throw you?

Or will it be the younger consumers who you mistreated when they were in college when you socked them with overdraft and ATM fees?

And how will you promote your blog, and where are those funds going to come from? [Let me know when you've had enough, I could go on for hours].

Bottom line: Don't rush to blog, banks. You've got a lot of work to do before launching one.

But If You're Going To Blog....

A few recommendations to the growing list of firms jumping on the blogging bandwagon. If you're going to blog:

1) Sign the entries. A post on one firm's blog starts with "you won't believe what was in my inbox." My reaction: Who are you? CEO? VP, Marketing? Someone else? Verity Credit Union of Seattle, WA provides a great example for firms to follow. It lists all the contributors to the blog on the site, and has the person who wrote a particular entry sign it. I'm sure that your readers want to know this.

2) Use pictures of your bloggers. A study done a few years ago found that real pictures of the people who work at a firm (not stock photos) raised site visitors' perceived trust of the firm. It will make blog visitors feel like they're communicating with a real person, even if they've never met him or her.

3) Post your comments policy. Whether or not you moderate comments, let people know on the main page. Toronto Electrical Utilities Credit Union does a great job of this on its blog. Its posted policy clearly lets people know how to enter a comment, and what to expect when they do.

4) Categorize your posts. Piedmont CU does a nice job of categorizing blog entries so visitors can find something from the archives if the category strikes a chord. The benefit of doing this right from the start is that it should give the CU's bloggers a beacon for what topics to write about.

5) No commercials. It's not what your blog is for, and you don't need them. Especially "ads" for online banking or other online services. I don't have data to support this contention, but I bet a lot of your blog's readers already bank online. And I bet they read the blog to connect with you — not get sold to.

☺ Banks And Credit Unions: Two Approaches To Blogging

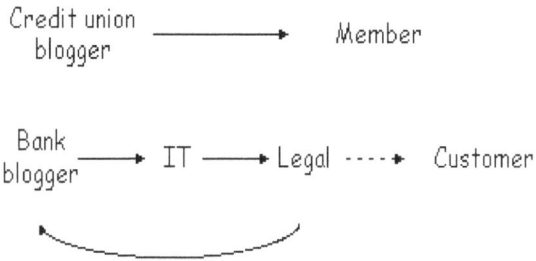

Credit union blogger ⟶ Member

Bank blogger ⟶ IT ⟶ Legal ┄┄➤ Customer

You can draw your own conclusions on which approach is more effective for engaging customers in a dialogue.

Whose Product Review Do You Trust?

It seems like every day someone comes out with a survey that shows that the most trusted source of opinions are our friends and family. My reaction: Duh. This has always been true. Web 2.0 didn't cause this — it only enabled the sharing of opinions.

One recent source of this data point is Forrester Research who found that 83% of consumers said that their most trusted source for a product review was the opinion of a friend or acquaintance that has used a product or service.

What's more eye-opening — and often lost in all the discussion about social media — is what came in at second place, cited by 75% of respondents: A review of a product or service in a newspaper, magazine, or on TV. Forrester doesn't report its data with a margin of error, but if it did, it's possible that these top two sources could be equally trusted.

Perhaps even more surprising, especially for the blogosphere, was that the least trusted source of information was an online review by a blogger, trusted by only 30% of respondents.

What it means:

- **User reviews don't replace expert reviews.** Forrester didn't break out their findings by demographics, but I'd guess that consumers over the age of 40 were the ones driving up the trust in newspapers, magazines, and TV. Marketers need to look at their existing (and target) customers' demographics to determine which sources of reviews will be most effective, from both an impact (change in buying intention) and cost (to collect and publish reviews) perspective.

- **Marketers need to bring it all together.** While Forrester's data suggest that social media sites would be a natural outlet for consumers to find and share reviews, it did find that 60% of respondents trusted reviews on a retailer's site. Site designers should incorporate various sources of reviews on their sites, and incorporate the types of trusted sources into the user personas that they define.

- **Buying bloggers' favors are fruitless.** A recent incident in which Microsoft allegedly incented bloggers to publish favorable remarks certainly backfired from a PR perspective. Forrester's data suggests that it wasn't an effective way to influence buyer intentions or behavior in the first place.

The Rules Of Viral Web Success (My Foot)

According to an Adweek article called The Rules Of Viral Web Success, At Least For Now:[35]

" ...the OfficeMax "Elf Yourself" campaign, which wrapped up last week, drew more than 110 million visitors. The secret [to its success]: Keep it dead simple, make it personal and give people a reason to pass it on. These sites might not win awards or wow other creative directors, but they draw big audiences by eschewing the urge to add on features and functions. "Digital agencies often get wrapped up in thinking it won't be interesting if they don't use the latest and greatest technology," said Daniel Stein, CEO of EVB. "That's a fallacy."

My take: This is the stuff that drives CEOs/CFOs crazy. Nowhere in the article does it mention metrics like incremental awareness, improved brand affinity, or [heaven forbid] incremental sales as measures of success. According to the article, Alexa ranked Elf Yourself as a top 1000 site in 50 countries. OfficeMax does business in five.

You want rules of viral web success? A viral web effort succeeds when it:

1) Attracts consumers relevant to your firm's product/service offering. According to OfficeMax's SVP of Marketing "Eighty-year-old women are sending these out and 8-year-olds are doing it." Great. But how many 80 year old women and 8 year old kids shop at OfficeMax or influence office supply purchases? Viral web efforts can be deemed successful when they connect with your firm's customers/prospects.

2) Is relevant to your business. Elf Yourself is great — I did it myself with my kids and sent it on to their grandparents who got a kick out of it. But I can't help but wonder how many of the 110 million visitors knew the site was sponsored by OfficeMax, or remembers a month later. Give OfficeMax credit for offering online deals in the middle of the experience, but that's not enough of a connection. Any business could have done Elf Yourself. A viral web effort is successful when it reminds participants of the sponsoring firm.

3) Supports the brand. If OfficeMax's brand positioning was the "fun place to get your office supplies" I'd be more willing to call a Elf Yourself a successful campaign. But in 2006/2007 OfficeMax launched a rebranding effort (with its new rubberband logo), promising an "efficient marketing model" with a "focus on efficiency and return". Elf Yourself doesn't really support these objective. A viral web effort is successful when it does support your firm's brand goals.

The problem isn't agencies getting wrapped up in the latest technologies, it's losing sight of the business goals and objectives. And you wonder why marketing is facing accountability issues?

The Anti-Web 2.0 Movement

He might not take this as a compliment, but I think Andrew Keen will be recognized as the Bill O' Reilly of the Anti-Web 2.0 movement.

Love him or hate him, O' Reilly accomplished something very important for the conservatives in this country: He defined the enemy. For a long time, many conservatives struggled to describe exactly who they had their disagreements with. Until O' Reilly came along and defined the term Secular Progressive.

In his Change This manifesto, Keen, the author of "The Cult Of The Amateur," does the same for the growing number of voices railing against the Web 2.0 movement.[36] In his manifesto, he defines the digital utopians, who, according to Keen, believe that:

"The mainstream media is an elite racket monopolized by privileged experts, which has failed (they believe) to reward real talent. Society is, consequently, full of unjustly published writers, unrecorded musicians, undistributed movie directors. Web 2.0's technology, therefore, is emancipating. By becoming bloggers and podcasters, we — the traditional audience — become the empowered author. [Web 2.0] technology frees culture from the traditionally authoritative [media] institutions. So the "good guys" — the bloggers, remixers, and denizens of the virtual worlds — are uniting audience and author into something called 'citizen media'."

Keen warns, however, that the greatest casualty of this vision is the "disappearance of shared cultural understanding and experience. Conversation — one of the ideological fetishes of the Web 2.0 movement — is one of the first casualties. In a world of 70 million bloggers publishing 1.5 million blogs in the US every day, we are too busy broadcasting our opinion to have anything to say to each other."

Keen is not alone in his critique of the Web 2.0 movement. John Dvorak of PC Magazine recently wrote:

"Every single person working in the media today who experienced the dot-com bubble believes that we are going through the exact same process and can expect the exact same results—a bust. The current bubble, called Bubble 2.0 to mock the Web 2.0 moniker, is harder to pin down insofar as a primary destructive theme is concerned. A number of unique initiatives, however, are in play here."

Dvorak goes on to list a number of aspects of Web 2.0 that may contribute to its destruction, including "neo-social networking", "mobile everything", and user-generated content.

My take: Both Keen and Dvorak are wrong on certain counts, but raise valid points on others:

▪ Conversation is not a casualty of the Web 2.0 movement. In fact, in terms of business-to-customer conversations, firms haven't even begun to scratch the surface of what's possible. What Web 2.0 has done, is given more people a way for their voice to be heard — even if nobody hears it, and even if that voice isn't worth hearing (although that judgment would be a display of the same eliteness digital utopians are guilty of).

▪ Dvorak (who I believe was intentionally fanning the flames by overstating the unanimity of the media in expecting a bust) is wrong to characterize the current Web 2.0 environment as a bubble. The dot-com era was a bubble in that the mania that overtook business pushed up stock prices to ridiculous levels. But current stock market prices aren't buoyed by Web 2.0 fever. Hence, no Web 2.0 bubble.

But both men are right in identifying an irrational exuberance with the current and potential impact of Web 2.0. This irrationality is nothing new — generations have overstated, overpromised, and over-hoped for the impact of their particular social revolution going back to Marx (Karl, not Groucho).

My bet is that the truth lies somewhere in the middle. Web 2.0 will have significant impact on some aspects of how we interact from both a interpersonal and business perspective — but not all of the current Web 2.0 technologies will contribute equally. And it might take so long for those changes to take hold, that it will hardly seem like a revolution.

Most important, however, is that these guys represent what is becoming the Anti Web 2.0 movement — Keen in particular, with the publication of his book. And even if you don't agree with them — and the other voices rising up in opposition to Web 2.0 — they're worth listening to and considering. They learned something from the last bubble (and possibly even those previous to that). And you might learn something from that.

The Devolution Of Social Networking

The marketing blogosphere is awash with bloggers falling over each other proclaiming social networking the next greatest thing since sliced bread. So I found this comment on Currency Marketing's blog site intriguing:[37]

"Social networking takes on different forms. One is the web, the other is talking to customers, regularly, all the time, everyday."

There's a growing number of marketers trying to introduce new technologies and — more importantly — new ways to interact with and engage customers. But what's a skeptical senior executive to think if the term social networking applies not just to applying new technologies and approaches to communication, but to the same old ways of talking to customers, all the time, everyday?

One conference speaker's experience helps to highlight the potential danger here. Regarding the Social Networking portion of a recent Net Finance conference, William Azaroff, who helped pioneer Vancity Credit Union's online community at ChangeEverything.ca commented that "many people came up to me, but many more had gone home." Ted Josephson opined that "a reason the traditional bankers left was due to general ignorance of the Social Media phenomenon's impact."

My take: If social networking is "talking to members, regularly, all the time, everyday", you can't blame them for leaving early.

It's too soon in the evolution of social networking for its definition to become diluted and co-opted. Proponents need to work to distinguish the approach (not just the technologies) from traditional ways of interacting and communicating with customers.

How to do this? One idea: When making presentations at meetings and conferences, include what I call the "Stuart Dopey Graphic", affectionately named after a former boss (named Stuart, duh). A SDG graphic has two columns and anywhere from four to six rows. The two columns were labeled "today" and "future", and the rows are attributes that help to distinguish how the future is clearly different from the past. Putting together this graphic is not as easy as it sounds.

But it's a step towards helping skeptical execs see how social networking is different from what banks and credit unions have done in the past.

☺ Why Web 2.0? Why Not NGW?

Computer programmers of the previous century, in an attempt to save time and disk space, used to leave off the first two digits of the year when creating date fields. This, of course, turned out to be a bad decision.

Instead of being referred to as the Year 2000 problem, it become known as Y2K. Three characters instead of nine (including the space). Which is ironic, because it was that kind of thinking that got us into trouble in the first place.

Given this predilection, it's odd that the term "Web 2.0" has become so widely adopted. Granted, it's only seven characters (again, with the space). But surely, the technocrati could have done better than that.

Why not NGW (next-generation web)? Or NMI (new millenium Internet)? Even Web 21 (evoking the 21st century, get it?) is shorter by one character.

Of course, if Apple had its way, we'd have iWeb. Left to General Motors, and it would have been NYFI (not your father's Internet). And thank god we didn't let Microsoft name the concept. Otherwise, we'd be talking about Web 2002 (10.6832.6830) SP3.

But Web 2.0 is what it is. I'll bet you this, though: That Tim O'Reilly is watching this like a hawk, just waiting for the right time to proclaim the start of Web 3.0.

EPILOG: CLOSING THOUGHTS

Management Religion Versus Management Science

Tim Keiningham has noted that:

Managers adopted NPS with the presumption that it was grounded in solid management science."

My take: That's not necessarily true. It should not be a foregone conclusion that managers adopt NPS — or any management approach, for that matter — because they believe it is grounded in management science.

For better or worse, managers often put their faith in a management technique's promise to deliver results simply because it fits with their view of how the business world works — and for no other reason besides that.

In other words, the management technique becomes their management religion.

The business world sees these religions come and go all the time. Today it's NPS, in the past it was knowledge management, growth (remember the book "Grow To Be Great"?), and reengineering. What often underlies these theories, methods, and approaches isn't solid management science but persuasive, engaging, correlative, and anecdotal writings from consultants, management authors, and the growing cadre of consultainers.

There's nothing inherently wrong with advocating for, or believing in, any particular management religion. But adherents can fail to objectively assess the shortcomings and weaknesses of their chosen religion.

But unlike the real world, where a certain set of beliefs may guide someone for a lifetime, management religions may only be appropriate for a limited time.

Changing management religious views, however, is often difficult for adherents. They've made big bets in terms of money and reputation. It often takes disruptive upheavals (not to mention new management) to make it happen.

There are lessons here for both sides of the coin: Management scientists shouldn't expect managers to adopt their recommendations and techniques just because there is sound management science behind their theories. That's not how managers manage. Interestingly, it's the scientists who understand better than anyone that our decisions are guided more by emotion than reason.

But on the other hand, management zealots need to take a less protective view of their [often] new-found religion. Correlation does not mean causation. One size doesn't fit all. These folks need to take a more tempered view and recognize that organizations differ, strategies differ, conditions differ, etc. and that they're approach simply isn't right for everybody..

I'm Sorry For This Lousy Book, I Know I've Let You Down

A number of observers have said that JetBlue's handling of its 2007 Valentine's Day crisis (specifically, ex-CEO David Neeleman's apology) will go down in marketing history as a case example of how to respond in a customer service crisis.

Marketing Daily, meanwhile, reported that Home Depot's new CEO gave "an unusually candid, plain-talking apology to readers of MSN Money."[38] According to the publication, Frank Blake said:

"There's no way I can express how sorry I am for all of the stories you shared. I recognize that many of you were loyal and dedicated shoppers of The Home Depot … and we let you down. That's unacceptable."

So this is the new marketing. No chest-thumping, "we're better than everyone else" claims of superiority. Apparently, the way to win over today's consumers is to bow your head in humility and confess your sins. It conjures up images of Jimmy Swaggert all over again.

Few firms are going to get away with this. What made the apology work for JetBlue was Neeleman's sincerity. I (and I'm sure, many others) believed that he was truly sorry. And as the founder and [still] CEO of the company, Neeleman's imprint and DNA are still all over the company. So we believe the company is sorry. And because many of my past experiences with the company have been positive, many of us will accept the apology and give the firm another chance.

But are Home Depot customers as willing to accept the new CEO's apology as readily? No way, and here's why: He hasn't earned the right to ask for our forgiveness. The actions of his firm don't sync with his apology. In short, it won't come off as sincere.

And that's the new marketing weapon — sincerity. It's why -- and how -- small firms compete, and ultimately topple, larger firms. Because they're perceived to be sincere when they claim to be an advocate for the customer (not the other way around), and claim that they want to help their customers manage their lives. It's hard for many people to believe firms' claims when they're hit with snowballing fees or impersonal service.

Doing business with — and being loyal to — a firm is a relationship. And we want relationships with people and firms we believe to be sincere about wanting a relationship back. This isn't easy stuff. You have to earn it — you can't simply make the claim that you're sincere in your next marketing campaign.

And that's why I'm so cynical about the Marketing 2.0 revolution. It doesn't replace the need for sincerity and authenticity. And more importantly, the developments in technology that we've seen over the past ten years didn't create the need for these attributes. They've always been there.

Groucho Marx said it best: "The best way to create loyal customers is through honesty and fair dealing."

He said that some sixty years ago. What was true then is true today. Groucho being Groucho, however, he did go on to say: "If you can fake that, you've got it made."

So let me say this: I am truly sorry for the lousy quality of this book. I promise to never let it happen again. In fact, I'm going to publish a Bill of Rights that will guarantee you high quality in all my future books.

But if you think there's going to be financial recompense for buying this one, keep dreaming.

About the Author

Ron Shevlin has been a marketing consultant and executive for nearly 25 years, but doesn't look nearly as old as that sounds. Since the authors of other marketing books feel compelled to mention it, it goes without saying that Ron has consulted to some of the leading financial services, consumer product goods, retail, and manufacturing firms in the world. Contact Ron with your comments at ron.shevlin@gmail.com.

NOTES

[1] Forrester Research, "Inbound Marketing Goes Mainstream", September 19, 2005.

[2] Direct Magazine, "How Non-DMers Measure Up", April 1, 2007.

[3] Marketing Profs, "Marketing-Led Organization -- Or Bust", December 2006.

[4] AdWeek, "CMOs Left In The Lurch", April 16, 2007.

[5] Forrester Research, "The Evolved CMO", http://www.forrester.com/imagesV2/uplmisc/The_EvolvedCMO.pdf.

[6] Harvard Business School Working Knowledge, "Fixing The Marketing-CEO Disconnect", May 21, 2007.

[7] Forrester Research, "Want To Nurture Next-Generation Marketing Skills?", August 7, 2007.

[8] http://tinfoiling.wordpress.com/2007/10/03/3-days-of-highlighted-points/.

[9] http://blog.jimnovo.com/2007/08/15/customer-marketing-testing/.

[10] http://www.webanalyticsdemystified.com/weblog/2007/02/myth-of-actionability.html.

[11] http://semphonic.blogs.com/semangel/2007/02/all_the_worlds_.html.

[12] Harvard Business Review, "Understanding Customer Experience", February 2007.

13

http://customerexperiencematrix.blogspot.com/2007_01_01_archive.html.

14

http://marketingbytesman.typepad.com/my_weblog/2007/03/when_banks_go_b.html.

[15] http://marketingroi.wordpress.com/2007/03/06/wow-way-over-wrated/.

[16] http://www.kaushik.net/avinash/2007/10/engagement-is-not-a-metric-its-an-excuse.html.

[17] Target Magazine, "The Skinny On How Marketers Will Be Spending Their Direct Response Media Budget", March 1, 2007.

[18] Ad Age, "What's The Value Of An Engaged Viewer?", July 9, 2007.

[19] http://www.cscape.com/features/Pages/customer-engagement-register.aspx.

[20] Harvard Business Review, "How Valuable Is Word Of Mouth?", October 2007.

[21] http://blog.jimnovo.com/2007/06/19/lifecycle-ltv/.

[22] http://blog.jimnovo.com/2007/05/17/ltv-engagement/.

[23] Journal Of Marketing, "A Longitudinal Examination of Net Promoter and Firm Revenue Growth", July 2007.

[24] http://customeru.wordpress.com/2007/12/11/giving-senior-executives-more-insight-from-nps/.

[25] Marketing Letters, "The Consumer As Advocate: Self-Relevance, Culture, And Word-Of-Mouth.

[26] Forrester Research, "Demystifying The WOM Consumer", October 30, 2007.

[27] DM News, "Passionistas Are Engaged, Loyal Advocates: Yahoo Study", September 26, 2007.

[28] http://www.bubblegeneration.com/2007/12/apple-edgeconomy-and-future-of.cfm

[29] http://mitsloan.mit.edu/faculty/pdf/trustbased.pdf.

[30] University of Washington news.org, "Emotional, Not Factual, Ads Win Skeptical Consumers, Study Shows", August 15, 2005.

[31] Forrester Research, "The ROI Of Blogging", January 24, 2007.

[32] http://www.useit.com/alertbox/articles-not-blogs.html.

[33] Jupiter Research, "Blogs And Banks", June 12, 2007.

[34] http://www.thebankchannel.com/2007/08/banks-urged-to-open-blogs.html.

[35] Adweek, "The Rules Of Viral Web Success, At Least For Now", January 7, 2008.

[36] http://www.changethis.com/35.03.AgainstYou.

[37] http://www.currencymarketing.ca/index.cfm?method=blog.BlogDrilldown&blogentryid=367d382a-a96e-0577-aec5-8690494fe36f.

[38] Marketing Daily, "Home Depot Offers 'Mea Maxima Culpa', Latest In A Line", March 15, 2007.

Acknowledgements

In addition to my wife and daughters, to whom the book is dedicated, there are a few people who deserve my thanks for this project.

Thanks to Michael Della Penna, David Aordkian, and Gene Blishen who reviewed drafts of the manuscript and provided invaluable feedback.

I'd also like to thank my Twitter friends (if you don't know what that means, you'll have to go online and figure it out for yourself). Most of these folks read and comment on my blog. Their conversation, input, and feedback really drove a lot of the content.

Last -- and definitely not least -- I want to thank Brent Dixon from Trabian for conceptualizing and producing the cover art. He made an investment of time and effort that I will find hard to repay.